NSTIWTIWGD

Skydivers' Stories

Written by

Skydivers Around The World

and

Compiled By

Tim Long
Doug Garr

These stories are dedicated to

the spirit of

BSBD

EFS

JLS

Cover illustrations by Robert Thundercloud
Used with permission of Tom Sanders (copyright owner)

Book Design and Layout by Janet Works

First Edition: Winter 2015
Reprinted As Needed (Print-On-Demand) 2018 +

ISBN 978-1726750950

Stories

Introduction

It is one of the most endearing traits of skydivers the world over. We tell each other stories about what happened…up there…where most reasonable folks are afraid to venture. Sometimes what happens is harrowing or funny or harrowing and funny at the same time. Mostly, harrowing. These slices of time, just seconds or minutes, tend to blur over the years. But those jumps where something went horribly wrong are the ones that are forever indelible in our memories many years later.

I had been wondering where the expression that is the title of this book came from. Like Beowulf, there is no known author. We do know that when skydivers sit around the bar or the bonfire, and someone begins a tale with "No shit, there I was, thought I was gonna die…." the ensuing story will be met with some combination of wonder, shock, laughter and derision. After a NSTIWTIWGD declaration, attention must be paid.

Still, I wondered. Back in 1989 *Sports Illustrated* published a long article about the special relationship between two skydivers, Mike Sergio and Owen Quinn. Mike's claim to fame was doing one of the great outlaw demos of all time, jumping into Shea Stadium at night during the 1986 World Series between the Red Sox and the Mets. Ten million baseball fans remember Mookie Wilson's ground ball going through first baseman Bill Buckner's legs, a Little League error that cost the Sox the sixth game and ultimately the Series.

Ten thousand skydivers, however, remember Mike doing a standup on the first baseline between innings. Sergio told me later that it was not a big deal. How could you miss a drop zone that big, lit up that brightly? Hardly a high pucker factor leap in his view. But Owen Quinn's jump, that was something else. About a decade earlier, Mike had helped Owen plan a BASE jump off the World Trade Center, another of the most spectacular bandit jumps of all time. Now that was one hairy-ass stunt, because in the 1970s not too many folks were jumping off fixed objects, let alone into downtown Manhattan. Had I known about it in advance, my advice might have been something like, "Dude, no shit, I think you're gonna die." (He used a round, and no sleeve to ensure a faster opening. The spring-loaded pilot chute was seated with a copy of *Reader's Digest* instead of a conventional kicker plate, which Owen thought might hit somebody on the ground.)

Anyway, there was nothing special (to a skydiver, that is) about *Sports Illustrated's* thesis that went beyond "Wow, these two guys actually knew each other and were good friends." But here is how it relates to NSTIWTIWGD: The writer began his story with the following anonymous quote, "No kidding, there I was!" He'd probably heard the full length, unexpurgated exclamation, but the editors wisely decided to reduce it to the PG version because, after all, it is a family sports magazine. He went on to say that every story began the same way, NKTIW.

* * *

In the following pages you will find dozens of tales that begin somewhere up in the wild blue yonder and end on terra firma, usually happily and without injury and/or death. On some of the scarier ones, your eyes will boggle and your armpits will get dewy. Be gratified that it is not you who needs a change of underwear. Of course, some of them do not rate much more than a ho-hum, or meh, and some of them occurred on the ground. We'll leave that to the reader to decide. The important thing is that in each of these stories, its narrator unleashed that notorious gremlin of terror or fear in every parachutist's brain that is scratching the anterior lobe: *"Hmmm. I wonder if this one is going to be the last one."* There are some skydivers that do not subscribe to this theory. Either their emotional cortex is empty, or they are liars.

When Tim Long and I edited these stories, we decided that the threshold for inclusion would be relatively simple. The single most important element was that the person regaling us with his or her tale convinced us that the gremlin was scratching pretty hard at some point during the actual jump.

Only a very few skydiving stories were rejected. I tossed out one of my own, for example, describing a CRW skydive on which I found myself open at about 15,000 feet and a 747 on approach to JFK passed me at altitude about a mile off to my left. My initial thought was, well, this is not very comforting. But it happened so quickly, I never thought I could have died until well after I thought I could have died. Slight discomfort does not make a NSTIWTIWGD story.

The ideal tale is one that I extracted from Mike Sergio, who I mentioned earlier. It's a story I remember him telling me after we discussed the Shea Stadium jump. Basically, it's a story of four skydivers losing altitude awareness at the same time. This in itself is not that uncommon. But when he saw Scotty Carbone, a skydiver who was well known for taking it off the bottom, dump in the middle of the formation, it flashed through his mind that it was all over. Almost everyone who has had the experience of jumping with Scotty knew that if you pulled lower than he did, then you were probably going in.

For Tim, it was Randy Forbe's rattlesnake dive, which made him laugh, and Criss Morgan's, which made him sweat, that capped this collection of stories that most of us who jumped in the 1960s to the 1980s can relate to. They are a part of this great lifestyle called skydiving.

From the adrenaline of seeing a friend survive to taking part in a DZ prank or two, these stories bring back that era to us like none other. These are not for the whuffos; they are for the few of us that know the singular joy of flying.

Somewhere My Star
(sung to the tune of "Laura's Theme")

Blue skies above,
And green, green earth below,
The wind in my face,
My friends flying in.

Flying so free
Halfway to the heavens.
Hands linked with hands
A star is born anew.

Tim and I are certain that you will find stories in this modest book you can identify with. Philip de Louraille, a skydiver who teaches astronomy in California, contributed my own favorite. It concerns a BASE jump he made long ago that went terribly awry. When I read it I thought that nothing would ever top that one. Re-reading it still has me shaking my head, wondering how he survived, moistening up my armpits.

That we lived to tell these tales, and exaggerate them if necessary, is this book's *raison d'etre*. We hope you enjoy it.

Doug Garr

Bare-Ass and Up a Tree

I did all the No-Nos: I was not current, I had borrowed gear, and I was naked. But how could I pass up a chance to do a BWSCR record? ("B" as "in-the-buff.") It was to be the biggest Naked-Lady load to date, so I went.

We built the formation and everything was working fine until pull-time. I pulled and waited…nothing. I reached around again and felt the hand-deploy still tucked into its pouch. Tossed that and waited…nothing. Then I looked up and around, elbowed the container…nothing.

About then the adrenalin in my body and the alarm in my head sent me grabbing for the reserve handle. My left hand grabbed and I gave my left hand a hard punch with my right, which put my hand-mounted altimeter right in front of my eyes. It read straight up ZERO.

Time kind of stopped right then. I was peacefully aware of a pillow of green and the perfectly round tops of several phone poles rising beneath me. The mountains to the East were eye-level, the afternoon sunlight golden. It registered that I was about to die. I remember thinking: "Well, it's not going to hurt."

That's when I got line stretch with just enough time to cross my legs and arms as I sank into an enormous green tree. I landed seated on a branch and listened to twigs and leaves crackling down to the lawn below.

Then an old lady came out the front door of the house, looked up, and asked me if there was something she could do to help me. I said, "Yes ma'am, you can get me some clothes because I don't have any." She said, "Oh my God, you don't!" and went back in the house.

Immediately a car zoomed up. Several guys from the DZ jumped out, threw me and the gear in the car, and we headed back to the DZ.

About half an hour later, the Elsinore police arrived at the DZ to investigate a report of a naked lady landing in somebody's tree. At least 100 people saw me freefall past that tree line an hour before, but somehow nobody knew a thing about any naked ladies. The bemused cops left and another NSTIWTIWGTD story was born.

Hindsight note to self on borrowed gear: It would have been useful had I remembered that a main ripcord handle is not in the same place as a hand-deploy, but a cut-away handle is.

Marilyn Perrine Wuest added this postscript: "The weekend after Sandy landed in the tree, I was teaching a First Jump Course; I always asked the students what brought them out to Elsinore to jump. One gentleman told me that the previous weekend he was driving by and saw a naked woman hanging in a tree. One look at that and he decided he was definitely going to try this sport."

Sandra Doyle Drahman

High Wire Act

Down at Otay one nice day, Jim Salzer, Bobby Bender and I made a jump from 7,500 feet and until it became a NSTIWTIWGD experience, it was a totally unremarkable jump.

We ended up down at the east end of the DZ. As I turned down-wind (to circle around the gas truck) and then turned back into the wind, I was going faster than when I turned downwind. I was a 100-jump wonder at the time, but I still knew enough that something strange was happening.

The winds kicked up to 35 knots or so. I was on a PC screaming backwards toward the hill (berm) at the end of the DZ. Salzer landed about 50 feet before the hill and got dragged. I was looking back, getting ready to hit the rocks, and suddenly I found myself airborne and swinging around the wires that run parallel to the hill. Like a gymnast, I grabbed the wire as I was coming around and got my hands twisted up.

Both of my Capewells were on the wire and the canopy was now pulling me down the wire to where it turns 90 degrees and starts wrapping around another wire. I looked back and actually saw people looking at me.

I asked if someone could get me down. Next thing I knew, Ed Miller climbed up the pole, grabbed my chest strap and did a curl. He released my Capewells and helped me climb down the pole.

Poor Bobby actually hit the rocks and got pretty banged up. My face scraped the wire and it took off quite a few of my freckles, but nothing too damaging.

I don't remember who got my canopy down off the wires. Bill Deli said he actually saw footage of this fiasco at a later date. He still has the risers from that harness, too.

Chris Deli Schilpp

Earth

For the 4th of July celebration at the Bartlesville Country Club in Oklahoma, we were going to make a demo jump just after the fireworks display ended. I was jumping a 28-foot 7-TU that I had further modified by cutting out a panel. My reserve was a 26-foot conical. This was my 202nd jump. In another month I would buy a PC. Since we wanted to jump *after* the fireworks display—not during it—we established ground communication with some sort of portable radio on the ground at the club.

We circled the landing area in the Cessna 172, watching the fireworks until they called for us after the finale. The smoke from the fireworks indicated the wind was blowing from a different direction than it had been during daylight hours. Actually the wind had not switched; it had just died below a few hundred feet like it usually did on summer nights. Jerry Henshall, the jumpmaster for the load, told me that the ground crew said the wind looked like it shifted completely around, but he wasn't sure. He asked me where I wanted to get out. I said "You decide," but forgot to add "Just tell me." I knew the area by daylight, but not at night.

I was last out of three jumpers at 5,600 feet, and for separation at night, I waited several seconds and opened high. I looked around and had no clue where I was, or even which side of the Country Club I was on. I could see car lights on a road, but I didn't know if the road was on the east or north side of the club. I saw a big black plowed field below and decided that would be a safe landing target. Fortunately, the wind blew me off it.

Fortunately, because what I did not know then was that it was a lake. I did not have any flotation gear, and if I had landed there Cliff Davis would be writing this. Luckily, the "plowed field" was not an option. I decided to head for the car lights on the road. The wind was blowing that way anyway and I could get a ride back to wherever the country club was. I landed a couple hundred feet off the road, and just after I landed I looked up and saw the brake lights of a car flash. The car was just off the road when I landed.

I wrapped my parachute in my arms and ran up to the car. I was dressed in a red jumpsuit (red coveralls with patches) and wearing a black helmet with tinted bubble goggles, and I held a red and white parachute in front of me. A woman was in the car. She was not there to pick me up; she had parked there to watch the fireworks display.

I asked her, "Where am I?" She was speechless for several seconds and finally stammered, "Earth."

She was a cousin of the jumpmaster on the load, who did not make the Country Club either. He landed on a roof in a subdivision next to it. He was wearing a red jumpsuit and is somewhat over weight. Some wise ass drove by and yelled, "A little early for Christmas, fat boy."

Jerry L. Ward

This Is Way Safe

Oh my god. I bought a Strato-Star and my last jump on it was a BASE jump with it in a direct bag from the Gerald Desmond Bridge in Long Beach—165 feet into the water at night. That evil motherfucker, Mark Hewitt, talked me into going off backwards so that the photographer could get a better shot of my fear-filled face.

But as I launched, I threw my arms up for stability (or maybe in supplication) and all you saw was my right upper arm instead of my face. Just before I left, Mark, in all his evilness, leaned way out over the water while holding on to a suspension cable and said, "Don't worry, Scott, this is way safe."

When I hit the water, two guys went by in a sailboat under power and one of them was standing on the deck applauding me as he went by. No offer to help or assist—just a nice round of applause. I had to swim to shore with that rig in a special stroke Mark taught me that worked very well.

Scott Geil

Think I'll Have Another Beer

My scariest moment was on August 14, 1974.

After a two-way from 8,500 feet, I had a floating ripcord so, with such a wealth of experience, I pulled my chest-mounted reserve that decided not to open right away. I had to hand-feed the reserve and didn't have a good canopy until about 500 feet AGL.

So what's that, about three seconds left to the ground? My two boys witnessed this episode. No wonder they weren't that pleased with my chosen sport. Think I'll have another beer.

Sally Lacy

A Harrowing Night on the Troll

August 11, 1981. I am on top of the Trollveggen in Norway, one of the most famous BASE launch pads on the planet and one of the tallest mountains in Europe. I am the only one jumping that day, but I have five or so locals who made the ascent with me. This is my second try, having been fogged out previously. A few days before, two cars full of French guys drove from southern France to Lyon and then straight to Åndalsnes, a small town near the mountain from which I'm about to leap.

Fifty-two jumpers had previously stepped off this spot when I got up there (there's a logbook on top.)

Somewhere around 2 p.m., I am equipped and ready to go. I have a Super-8 camera on my head, filming backward. I have two people taking pictures to the right and left of the launching point. I am nervous! This is only my second BASE jump (my first was off El Capitan) and I am with total strangers. Nevertheless, I finally quiet the demons that are reminding me I'm out of my mind and step out into space—alas, forgetting to turn on my camera.

The launch off The Troll, as it is affectionately called, is very small. As you face the step-off spot, the mountain keeps on going up to your left and your right. Both sides go up for another 500 feet. The rock is not like El Cap. This is a dark rock, quite friable. At the bottom of the cliff, there is a huge pile of debris. This rock gets wet a lot and the temperature gradient between day and night is huge. So during the night (mostly) rocks fall off from the cliff (as the water in the rock turns to ice, expands, and loosens some of the rock.) Falling rocks smack themselves below and end up augmenting the debris pile.

Jumping there is like jumping off a half-cylinder, with walls on three sides of you.

So I step off and launch, just as I did on El Cap, building speed and getting that exhilarating feeling of "taking off" from the rock—which is created by the illusion of falling vertically yet moving away from the cliff by tracking.

Time to open! Pilot chute is out, bag is out, nice deployment but for the fact that the bag starts spinning! By the time the main is fully opened, I have three line twists.

I have time to undo one twist so at least I see where I am going, which is straight toward the cliff. Even though the brakes are still stowed, I'm moving toward the wall at a pretty good clip. Okay, I am going to hit the rock. Quick thinking tells me to present my right knee first to absorb the initial collision, then my right elbow, then my head. Bing, bang, bong. It hurts a bit but frankly, this is the last thing on my mind! The parachute is flying (falling?) forward toward the cliff and my face is now right there. I flip on my back and am moving straight down. The main is still open but is not controllable; I can't turn it. I am "falling" pretty darn fast. My back is against the rock, I can feel most of its outcrops as they whiz up. I stretch out my arms to avoid being flipped, and my speed increases.

I go into full *"fuck fuck fuck fuck fuck…"* mode for a little while until I see that I am about to stop going vertically down as the cliff is angling in a temporary 60-70 degree slope. I look farther down and see that I am about to go fully vertical again, but the canopy is now a mess. That transition slowed me down, and the bottom of the parachute is almost on top of my head. Some of the lines are getting over my arms and hands. I am thinking that if I am going fully vertical again, it may not open enough to slow me down.

Then the canopy falls over me.

Now I know I am stuck in the middle of a huge cliff attached to a big mountain: a proverbial ant lost on a hill. I am furious. I've never been so angry in my entire life. No euphoria is coming to blow my mind but an incredible rage. I shout at the top of my lungs: "I AM NOT SUPPOSED TO BE HERE, GODAMMIT!"

Time to assess my situation. I am stuck on a ledge that is about six feet long and a few inches wide. Wide enough for one foot to parallel the cliff, so perhaps six inches wide. I am not 90 degrees vertical but perhaps 70 degrees, so I have a slight slope to rest against. I can't really move—just those darn six feet forward or backward, but I can turn (resting my right or left shoulder against the cliff.) I can see way ahead and below, but I can't see the critical few feet ahead of me where the cliff goes vertical again. So I do not know if I can jump from where I am. The rock is slippery. If I step off that ledge, I may slide uncontrollably. *Fuck.*

From where I am, I can see the entire valley below. The view is fantastic. The parking lot where I was supposed to land is a tiny grey spot surrounded by green (and a road leading to it.) I can hear road noise coming from way below as cars, buses and trains pass below. Because I can see so much, I figure I am invisible from the landing zone point of view.

By then it is early afternoon. The good thing is that people saw me jump. I was not by myself, unlike two days before when I was considering jumping on my own when I was at the top but was fogged in. I think: *"They did not see my parachute go away from the cliff so they know I am stuck down there somewhere. It will take them five or six hours to get down and call for help. I'll know when help comes because the parking lot where I was supposed to land is the only spot where cars can stop."*

There was no wind, but I knew it could come up. I did not want to be dragged down by a burst of wind so I decided to pack my Hobbit back in my SST-Racer. One arm-length at a time and very carefully, I folded the fabric back in the bag, stowed the lines, and having my pull-up cord looped on my pants, I closed the rig so I could rest it on the ledge. That took about an hour. I checked my helmet and noted that the camera was not broken (it was facing backward.) That's also when I realized it was not turned on. *Shit.*

That would have been interesting footage! (Actually when I got the film developed, the initial impact did turn the camera on! But it was off when I first inspected it and as I write this, I do not remember how much of my descent got filmed. But I have that footage somewhere.)

I decide to pass the time by filming my situation. Where I am and where I was supposed to land.

Since it is summer and the location is high in latitude, I know it won't get dark until 10-11 p.m. and if the weather is nice the next morning, it will be clear by five a.m.

I have no water and no food and no lights. I am wearing a jumpsuit, a pair of shorts and a T-shirt underneath, and my rig and helmet. No watch. I am thinking that if the wind does pick up, perhaps I will unpack the chute, carefully lay it behind me as I move on that slippery rock ahead, and leap. Hopefully, it will inflate. Well, at least it's a plan.

Time passes and I notice that there are more and more cars in the parking lot, and the daylight is starting to fade. A helicopter arrives and lands in the parking lot. Aha! Things are getting interesting. Good thing I packed the chute, I think. I would not want the wind from the blades to throw me further down the rock. After a while the chopper lifts off, turns on its bright search light, and starts looking for me by climbing a little and moving in an arc.

I lost sight of the chopper, although I heard it slowly but surely making its way up. I could see it 50 feet below me when it turned around and headed back to the parking lot. It is too dark and I cannot signal to them that they were close. Now I know I am going to spend the night on that very small spot. The temperature, which was never very warm to begin with, is dropping and I start shivering—and shivering some more.

After a while I unpack the main and wrap it around me for a modicum of protection from the fog that has returned. The humidity is making the low temperature even lower. I know I can't fall asleep. There is no room for a mistake: one wrong move and down I go.

More time passes. I am very cold; I am also hungry and thirsty and quite miserable. I spend the time meditating that I am warm, and this helps a little.

At what must be two or three in the morning, I hear a big crack above and then a whistling sound that is increasing in volume and pitch.

Oh fuck. A big piece of rock is dropping. I do not know if the rock will miss me by falling right or left or a bit ahead or behind. I also have no clue how high it was when it cracked but it fell for quite a few seconds. Not knowing scares me. Because there is nothing I can do. If this rock is heading for me, then I am done. I become one with the cliff. I squish myself against the wall to present the smallest possible silhouette. I can feel in my right cheek the details of the rock it is resting against. I stretch arms and legs as I force myself to merge with the mountain. I am totally in that cliff. I do not remember breathing.

A big crash is heard from my left and a bit above, and I am showered by debris, mostly small stuff but hitting fairly hard. A few seconds later, the noise is much louder but below. The rock broke apart by hitting the cliff near me and by now has triggered a small avalanche. It takes a few minutes for the silence to return and for my heart rate and breathing to return to normal.

Slowly the darkness recedes and I begin to see the bottom of the valley. A little while longer and the cars come back to the parking lot and the helicopter is getting warmed up. Things are looking up. I repack my main.

The helicopter finally takes off and within 15 minutes they spot me.

One of the occupants is getting ready to come down on a winch and I wave to him not to do that. It's safer to just send the harness down so I can attach myself and get out of there before causing another rockslide from the rotor wash. Much to his credit, I am understood! But he wants me to jettison my rig because an unexpected deployment could not only kill me but take the helicopter out as well. So I toss my SST Racer.

The harness comes down. I study it as it gets near me: it looks like a full body harness and within a few seconds, I attach it by stepping in the leg straps and snapping the chest strap. I then point my right arm up to the guy watching and off we go.

As the chopper gains horizontal speed away from the cliff, I can't help noticing that my body position is affecting a spin. I immediately compensate and the speed builds up; I am getting closer to the chopper as it flies faster. I notice they are not winching me up. After about half a minute, I am getting some serious horizontal wind blast and start to play with the relative wind. A little tracking, half a flip … I am back facing the ground. I play with my arms, swooping and tracking, swooping and tracking, half a flip here and half a flip there. And then I get a feeling I am being watched; I look up and two of the rescuers are looking at me with bulging eyes. One is taking pictures and the other is shaking his head while tapping his right index finger to his head. In Europe this is the standard body language to tell someone they are crazy. I do not care; I am laughing, I am happy. I know my troubles are over. The trip down the mountain takes five minutes.

We are nearing the parking lot; the chopper is now steady at 50 feet and they are winching me down. About 100 people on the ground are looking at me and I am waving like an idiot. I notice an ambulance is there; four paramedics are watching my descent and they have a body splint and stretcher ready. When I am low enough, of them grabs one leg and another grabs the other leg. The two other guys grab my torso. I tell them I'm fine, and they let go.

I did not want to be dragged to the stretcher, and the medics are indicating I should step into the ambulance. I refuse because all I want to do is thank the chopper rescue folks. I indicate that by making signs with my arms and hand and pointing at the chopper whose blades are still turning yet slowing down. When it is safe to move closer, I walk over and profusely thank them. Everyone laughs, everyone is happy; the media is having a frenzy moment.

The lady reporter says, "Your friends saw you jump yesterday, but they did not see a parachute open. You were found a thousand feet below the jumping point. The rescue helicopter personnel radioed that when they found you earlier, your parachute was still closed. How is it possible that you are not dead or injured?"

The people who saw me jump did not see the chute open, and since I flew toward the cliff they assumed I had died. They reported this fact to the police when they made it down the mountain that evening.

The rescue personnel thought they were searching for a body and that is why they stopped when night came. Like all new scary things, BASE jumping had first impressed the Norwegians (at that time, they had the only known second jumpable cliff, El Capitan being the first) but with me being the second "fatality" in one month, the mood was that this was a suicidal sport and why endanger rescue personnel and spend rescue money for "those guys"?

I forget how many interviews I gave (not too many Norwegian TV channels back then) but there were quite a few newspaper stories. I have a collection of all of them somewhere, including several I scanned.

The local police confiscated my passport, my jumpsuit, and my helmet. The jumpsuit and helmet were displayed in a museum in Åndalsnes for quite a few years. Maybe they are still there. The rig was never recovered. Where I had stopped on the cliff and thrown the rig was a path no mountain climbers had yet wanted to take on their way to the summit; the rock is too fragile.

Two days later the police chief returned my passport and winked that there was a train to Sweden leaving the station in an hour or so and that I should be on it. No problem.

Back in France a few days later, and after more interviews, the French jumpers who had accompanied me were, naturally, upset they had not stayed and waited for better weather. Back in Los Angeles, my story was too incredible and unbelievable to make it on the then-popular TV show, *"That's Incredible."*

I had some legal troubles. The Norwegian authorities wanted me to pay for the rescue (about US$15,000). I objected because they rescued mountain climbers without charging them. It is not that I was ungrateful, but once I was stuck on that spot, how was that different from rescuing a climber who had fallen or had an equipment failure?

Anyway, this dispute went all the way to their Supreme Court which ultimately decided with my position. I did not even pay for the lawyer. A Norwegian lawyer stepped up and took the case for a chance to argue in front of that court. As a result, if you climbed Trollveggen afterwards, there were plenty of signs saying that if you needed to be rescued from a BASE jump, you would be sued if you were asked to reimburse the cost and refused to do so. I'm not sure what their position is today, as this happened so very long ago.

Philip de Louraille

Nick Got All His People Out

In 1981 or so, Frank Mott started a DZ in Ramona, Calif., and I went to work for him as a newly-minted static-line jumpmaster. My first weekend we were fighting a pretty good 3,000-foot cloud cover with students backed up over two days. I went over for a walk and talk with our pilot of the C-182, and he thought we'd might be able to get on top and then find a hole to sling the students through. That sounded like a plan so I geared up, gear-checked, and loaded three first-jump students aboard.

We took off from the small dirt strip surrounded by orange groves and mountains, and stayed low until we came to the end of the overcast, which was a lot further away than we had estimated, but we climbed up over the clouds and came back toward the DZ.

I was looking out the door and knew we were still way west of the DZ and over some pretty high mountains. I thought if we kept going this way we'd come over the valley were the DZ was and then if we could find a hole, we'd be fine. My altimeter read 3,500 feet, but we were passing mountain ridges that were 3,000 ft. AGL, or just 500 feet below us.

I hooked up the first guy's static line, went through all the checks, and was pep-talking him when I looked out the door again, just hoping to see something familiar. (In hindsight, we were way past the point where I should have said, "This is stupid, let's turn around.")

Then through the mist I saw mountain tops I could almost touch and I remember thinking (like all good jumpmasters should) that this would be a lousy place for the engine to quit.

And it sputtered out right then.

We were out of gas. We'd lingered way too long. And the fuel gauges in that particular C-182 didn't work. I knew the pilot was sticking the tanks, figuring a quick hop over the DZ to three grand and back. He put the Cessna into a good 70-mph glide and we descended into the still-solid cloud tops. I knew we were still miles from the DZ, with really no good place to dead-stick land.

I was trying desperately to come up with my next move, and quickly decided we had to get out. I was kneeling between the legs of the first student with his static line already hooked up but we were in solid clouds and I couldn't, in good conscious, put him out into what could be a mountainside just below us. So I told him to get in the door and I waited. Either we'd all make it, I thought, or we'll all die, but I wasn't about to shove out a first-jump student without a clue.

We finally busted through the bottom of the overcast but just feet over the mountains. And, I'll admit, with the ink barely dry on my jumpmaster ticket, I was fighting the urge to freak out. But then I noticed something. We were descending across the grain of the mountain tops. It was valley, mountain, valley, mountain, valley, mountain and I realized this was just going to be a timing deal.

Now that were in the clear, I could see the valley holding the DZ in front of us. But there were a few mountain ridges between us and it. And I could see they were rising fast enough that there was no way in hell we'd make it there.

I tapped the first student out over a fifteen-hundred-foot valley with his main static line hooked up. I watched him open and commanded the second student to get in the door. But instead of putting him out on his main, I reached around and grabbed his chest-mounted reserve handle and shoved him out when we hit the next thousand-foot valley. Since we were in a good gliding descent, he cleared the tail easily and I got the last two students out the same way. They were all jumping cheapo rounds and reserves so I had some confidence they would survive any rough landings.

We were getting pretty low now and I knew both me and pilot still had to get out. I looked up at the pilot and said, "Come on, we're going." But his never having jumped before was kind of screwing him up. Just as I was about to leave him, he banked hard left and I looked out the door as we were now going with the grain of the terrain but descending into a valley. Then I saw what he saw. There was an oval dirt racetrack that looked flat from a thousand feet. But I knew it wasn't. It was a motocross track and full of hills and jumps. So I yelled, "Come on, we gotta go."

But he was adamant about staying, so I wished him luck and climbed out on the strut.

But now I had a problem. I'd been jumping a Wonderhog up until then, but just weeks ago I had bought one of John Sherman's new Racers. It was the slimmer, better version of his old SST rig. As a rigger, I'd actually never packed a Pop-Top Racer before. So the first time I did it, I thought *No, that's not right,* and repacked it. I was kind of sure I did it right, but now I thought, *Here comes the pudding.* I was way too low for my main so I hung off the strut with one arm and pulled the reserve handle with the other. My plan was if I didn't get pulled off, I was going down with the plane. I was about four hundred feet over the valley floor.

Another side issue was my reserve canopy. It was a brand new Pioneer Super 22, the first round reserve made from F-111 fabric. And when I purchased it from Audrey Jackman (who was working for Dean Westgaard at Elsinore) I said, "You gotta be kidding me, you can see through this shit!"

But both Dean and Audrey assured me that from now on, all reserve canopies would be made out of F-111. So now there I was. Thought I might die.

I watched my pilot chute launch over my shoulder but since the pilot was trying to squeeze all he could get out of his glide, I let go rather than risk fouling it up in the tail. I opened very fast and only had a chance to glance right and left before I crashed into a hillside. I never even got a chance to reach for the toggles. Thank God for John Sherman and his Pop-Top, and thank God for Pioneer parachutes.

I looked around but had no idea where I was. And I started to cry. Did I just kill a load of students? I wasn't scared anymore but I was frantic with worry.

Meanwhile, back at the DZ they knew how much fuel we had so they knew we were either safely down somewhere or we'd crashed. They launched a guy in an ultra-light and soon he found us. He flew 50 feet over my head, pointing out which way I should walk.

It took me about three hours to stumble down to a road and begin walking down. The DZ truck found me shortly after and I was so relieved to see my three students safely sitting in the back of the truck. We all had a pretty good hug session.

The pilot didn't make out so well. The inviting racetrack didn't do him so good and he pretty much tore off the wings before plowing into a dirt berm that messed him up pretty badly. He lived, but I don't think he ever flew again.

I never really thought about that episode much after it happened. I couldn't because it might have been the end of my jumping, too. It wasn't until some years later when it had become just another jump story told around the bonfire that I heard it again. I was just walking up near the end of it—in time to hear Frank Mott say, "But, Nick got all his people out."

And it made me cry again. And proud of myself for the first time.

Nick DiGiovanni

Suddenly, I Noticed the Ground

The first time was a packing error, my packing error. I was on a coached dive with Carol Knemeyer. I distinctly remember the look on her face as she hovered in front of me while I pulled and failed to get anything out. I got hold of the pud, pulled once, pulled twice, and felt nothing but resistance from the pin.

I remember looking for a second at Carol, feeling a bit surprised that this was actually happening, but knowing it's time to pull the reserve. I actually felt pretty calm about the whole thing. Did the look, reach, pull with both hands, stayed stable, and the next thing I knew I was looking at my round reserve and thinking "oh yeah, it's round." I believe I was under my reserve at around 2,200 feet because I had pulled high.

The landing was pretty uneventful except my legs started shaking violently once I hit the ground. Delayed reaction, I guess. Mostly though, I think I was proud and relieved that I had an emergency and managed to live.

Relax, this gets better.

The second time was also on a coached jump over Taft, about five or six jumps later. This one was a disaster. I was at an unfamiliar drop zone, flailing all over the place on the jump, and I lost track of the altitude! And then when I went to pull, I couldn't get the pin out. Again, I was more than surprised this time and have to admit a bit frazzled, given all the circumstances. But I managed to get the reserve out, only to find that my main was open as well. Apparently the deployment of the reserve had knocked the pin out, and the main went, too. Either that or I had actually pulled the pin and didn't think I had—I'm still not sure which.

I don't remember now where I was altitude-wise, but I was definitely lower than 2,000 feet. The main was completely clear of the reserve, and not yet in any kind of down-plane trajectory, and so this time I cut the main away. I landed near the water canal and then watched as the main canopy followed me, but directly into the water.

After this, people started approaching me about switching to a throw-out. I thought "No, I'm not going to give up yet. The last time was a freak thing; the chances of it happening again are slim to none, right?"

Wrong. This time, however, I was jumping the rigger's Racer pull-out since my main was still drying out and being inspected. Three or four jumps later I was back at Cal City. I was on my first four-way with Bob Celaya, Carol and Diane.

Like many beginners, I was terrible at relative work. I remember seeing them in the three-way formation, waiting for me to dock as I flailed to nowhere fast. I tracked off to pull and again, had pud in hand but the pin was not coming out. This time I was sure the pin was stuck, and I thought, *Are you kidding me? Again?* I got pissed off! So there I am having another high-speed mal, speeding toward the ground, yanking my pud over and over again because I was determined to get it pulled.

Suddenly I noticed the ground, stopped what I was doing, and went for the reserve. Got it opened and instantly knew that I was way low. After I landed, I told everyone on the ground that I was under the reserve at one thousand feet. It was actually more like 750. For some reason I thought one thousand didn't sound as bad. After this jump, I decided to switch to a pull-out.

I'm glad I had this experience early in my jumping career. I developed a healthy respect for the potential danger involved, the importance of making quick, sound decisions, and the safety aspect of it all.

Even though I had a pretty prevalent case of gear fear for about the next 100 jumps, in all my 800 jumps I don't think anyone would have ever referred to me as a complacent or unsafe skydiver. I always took the conservative route, and knew my gear inside-out. And forever after, I jumped a throw-out.

Stacy Giarrusso

Green Weenie

The late, great Bill Stage, SCR 5, told me of a jump he made on which when he went to open his main (a round) nothing came out. He punched it as best he could but … *nada*. So he rolled over on his back to open the belly chute.

It opened fine and he lay there watching a nice white reserve fall away from him. Somehow the connectors had come undone. He remembered thinking, "I just had the green weenie."

Then *bam!*—the main opened. The reserve ripping off had broken out the main. He always laughed about that green weenie thought.

Tim Long

B-52 Looks Big Up Close

No shit, there I was … thought I was going to die by getting sucked into the nacelle of a jet engine or freefalling through the wing or fuselage of one of the world's biggest airplanes.

Under certain wind conditions we were in their flight pattern, and it was fairly common to watch them fly right over the DZ. I'm very surprised that none of the old Perrisites have written about any close encounters they may have had with B-52s from March Air Force Base. Anyone who has ever jumped at Perris knows the air base is right up the road a piece, and air traffic was a constant part of skydiving in this part of California.

One of my most memorable jumps was on a Twin Beech load that included Bill Stage and Al Frisby, among others. We climbed to 12,500 feet, got on jump run, and built a nice eight-way star, when … there it was. I looked up in time to see a B-52 fly past the formation so close that I could see the silhouettes of the pilots sitting in the cockpit of the gigantic airplane. Two other jumpers also saw it, from the conversations we had once we got on the ground. If we had been a few hundred feet in that direction, we might have punched through that bomber. It shook me up pretty bad.

I bet Jim *"Flyin' W"* Wilkins could tell some tales about B-52s at Perris since he was a pilot and jumper there for so many years.

Criss Morgan

Watch Out For the Horny Gorilla

In June 1978, Bob Alspaugh, the DZ owner at Stroud, Okla., asked me to go on a trip to Lake Charles, La. He had made arrangements with a couple of local jumpers there to train some static-line students and he needed someone to pack T-10s and help with training. I had a whopping 60 jumps at that time, and this was a BFD. My little ego was soaring.

We flew down there in the 182, which was way over-grossed with Bob and I and the pilot (whose name I don't recall) and about six military surplus student rigs with belly-wart reserves. Not to mention a full load of fuel.

We arrived in Lake Charles on a Friday evening and stayed at the home of one of the local skydivers, Charles Ritchie. On Saturday we trained about six or eight locals and put them out on static lines. Later in the afternoon I went up with Bob and Ritchie to do a three-way.

My first rig was a conventional setup with an American Papillion in a Sierra container that was equipped with an over-the-shoulder blast handle ripcord. I had a high-mount belly-wart with a 24-foot tri-vent reserve. Bob had modified the Capewells to a sort of R-3 design, only instead of little plastic tubes to grab, there were little nylon tabs. In hindsight it was not a great design. My jumpsuit was a two-piece Brand X.

I thought I was hot shit.

The plan for the jump was to do a three-way star and then a horny gorilla. We went up to 7,500 feet, our normal jump altitude. The three-way built pretty fast and then we threw our legs to the center for the horny gorilla. I was base, so they both had grips on me. Of course, when the gorilla happens the fall rate really picks up and the altimeter needles start to flop around.

When I thought we were at about break-off altitude, I started to shake the grips. Charles and Bob looked at each other and then looked back at me and smiled. Ah, the fix was in! They just kept holding onto me and kept smiling. The more I struggled to get loose, the funnier they thought it was. I don't know what altitude we finally broke, but it was definitely below two grand. I rolled over and probably didn't even track before grabbing the blast handle.

Some of you from that era might remember that the American Pap had an annoying tendency to occasionally streamer and naturally, this kind of thing occurs when you end up going low. So I looked up and there's a streamer.

In the past I had had some success by shaking and spreading the risers, but my efforts were not successful this time. I assumed the cutaway position and grabbed for the canopy releases. I was able to get a good grip on one release tab but my fingers slipped off the other one, so with one riser released, I had a violently spinning ball of shit. I grabbed the other release tab with both hands and that's when the canopy finally released.

I did about two backflips and then fired the old belly-wart. The poor little worn out MA-1 pilot chute popped out and started to do a little dance up by my feet, because I was head down on my back. I gave it a swift kick and it finally took off and the reserve opened. I remember having a very short canopy ride and a hard landing.

When I got back to the hangar, the witnesses were all wide-eyed. They told me that the reserve ride had lasted about seven seconds, which would put me at about 100 feet or less when I got open. Basically, within a few seconds of impact. Some of them had already turned away so as not to witness the horrifying moment of my going in.

I remember being agitated for the rest of the evening and I blamed myself for not getting a clean cutaway. Bob and Charles were still very amused by the whole thing. Charles remarked, "Didn't that horny gorilla feel great? I just wanted to hold it all the way in, didn't you?"

Ah, the good old days.

Roy Buchanan

Going Down for the Third Time

June 5, 1960. My first water jump was into the Valley Forge Country Club swimming pool. Steve Snyder (D-5) flew the plane, and Bob Spatola (D-28) let me use his Telsan Turn (T-Slot) B-12 rig.

Getting in over the trees, wires and clubhouse was so intense that I never thought about getting out of my harness until I was sitting on the bottom of the pool in eleven feet of water.

I was able to get everything off of me, but picked up a couple of suspension lines on the way up. Before long I was hog-tied and needed help to get out of the water. Everytime I surfaced, the crowd cheered. Finally some kid pulled me to the side of the pool. It was a great experience.

Water landings were the leading cause of parachuting fatalities in the decade of the 1960s. I found out why on that jump.

Lee Guilfoyle

It Wasn't Looking Good

It was a gorgeous Saturday, and I needed to qualify for my D license. We were at Oneida Lake in upstate New York around 1970, and we just had a terrific day, well, jumping into the lake. We were all using rags and skydiving with just bathing suits, water gear, and no helmet. I landed near what I thought was the pickup boat, and the crew enthusiastically greeted me and hauled me in. They asked me if anyone else was landing, and then I realized that these were just day trippers in a cabin cruiser and weren't part of our group.

At night there was a luau on the beach, and I was asked on the demo load. Okay. Night jump, narrow beach front. I'm jumping a PC and I'm pretty good at accuracy, so this shouldn't be a problem. I had water gear, of course, but no lights. We were sort of freelancing it. I just remember that I exited last from the C-182, did a short delay and opened high. The prevailing wind almost always came off the lake, so I expected to be open over the black. But whoever was spotting took the jump run the wrong way. Or, they figured the winds were light and they took the jump run downwind, off the lake.

After I checked my canopy, I noticed that I was well inland already. The upstairs winds were a lot higher than the ground winds and, of course, nobody checked them because we were basically doing a demo and had taken off a few miles from the target.

It wasn't looking good. I wasn't making any headway, and I started looking for an alternate. All I saw were the lights of the town, and the usual streets, wires and trees. I unhooked my reserve on one side, and unhooked my chest strap and started with rear risers. Now I'm thinking, *Shit, I'll be sliced by a power line or crash into somebody's roof.*

At about a grand, which is basically "decision altitude" for an off-DZ landing, I got a little panicky. The lights indicated places where one shouldn't be landing, and the no lights were, well, just dark patches I was hoping was park land or some kind of open space. I couldn't find a backyard that even looked promising.

At about 500 feet I started making some headway as the wind died down. I had a few hundred feet to go to clear the last building and land on the beach where the X was next to the bonfire. WTF, I figured, just go for it. I cleared a couple of roofs by 15 or 20 feet and I picked up my legs to just get by a sagging high-tension line. My pulse was still racing when the spectators were back-slapping me as if I had planned the landing that close.

Doug Garr

Hanging Nude Around the Airplane

This was my worst, scariest, and most dangerous jump ever.

It was a demo into the Treehouse Nude Ranch in Devore, Calif., for the *Miss Nude USA Pageant* that they held every year. I was the only female member of Pat Moorehead's California Aerial Circus Parachute Team. When making the nude jumps I wore my gear and tennis shoes and my banner that read *"Miss Buff Diver"*.

It was a beautiful day in June or July of 1976. I had jumped into the pageant for a few years and it was just another nude demo for me, or so I thought.

We usually took off from Rialto Airport. Our pilot this year was Bob Jones. He was the only pilot I felt comfortable with besides Jim *"Flyin' W"* Wilkins. Of course I trusted all the pilots, but Jim and Bob made me feel the most comfortable, probably because out of my 997 jumps, they were the ones who flew me the most.

We had Pat Moorehead, Leroy Howe, Dave Quigley, Bill Hallam, Jerry Kinley and Ron Durham on the load that year. Usually I went out last so that all eyes would be on me—and the cameras, too. I was such a camera whore back then. Okay, I looked good naked at 110 pounds. That was with gear on, too. Maybe I weighed 105 and my gear back then was probably another 25 pounds or so. I jumped a piggyback.

At altitude everyone else bailed out, leaving me and Bob Jones, our incredible one-eyed pilot. I took the plane around for a solo pass. On jump-run I yelled for a cut, climbed out on the top rung of the ladder, turned to my right to dive, and suddenly felt a tremendous tug and incredible pain on my right leg. I got my bearings and looked up.

I was truly startled when I saw that I was hanging upside down from the ladder. Nude.

Apparently when I turned to jump, my right leg slipped and went through the rung and I was now hanging from the ladder. I looked in the plane and Bob was also shocked. He couldn't help me because he had to fly the plane. We were alone in this crisis. I just knew that I had to get my leg unstuck to get off the plane.

Millions of things went through my head. I couldn't land with the plane. So I got in position to do some pull-ups. It was the only option I could think of. If you can imagine yourself as a child hanging on the bars at school upside-down by your knees and then letting the left one go, that is the position I was in. Buck naked, too, plus the weight of my gear on that leg (which is my bum leg that I fractured in a car accident in 1970 before I ever jumped.)

I was really hurting now, and thinking my old fractured femur might snap. I prayed to God to give me strength to get off that ladder, and all the while Bob flew a straight jump-run from the Treehouse toward Glen Helen Regional Park, just a few miles away.

It was time to become Wonder Woman. I squared myself up the best I could and mustered every ounce of strength to pull myself up. I pulled up but couldn't even touch the ladder. Poor Bob was watching me struggle and by the look on his face, he was truly feeling helpless.

I tried again a couple of times, maybe more, and kept failing. My rig felt like it weighed a thousand pounds now. After about six tries I had no idea where we were and didn't really care; I was exhausted. I looked at Bob. Neither of us said a word; we just sent panicked, helpless glances back and forth.

I do know one thing for sure. Bob certainly had a good look at my bod.

Eventually I said to myself: *"I'm not going to die today."* I focused on what I needed to do: pull myself up high enough to grab at least one part of the ladder. If I can get hold of the ladder, I thought, I can inch my way up to the point where I could free my leg.

Finally, I did it and took hold of the ladder. I inched my way up, being very careful not to lose my grip. If that happened, I was done for. I got to the point where I could remove my leg, which by now was throbbing, from the ladder. I was in a lot of pain, but gave Bob one last look as I freed my leg and let go.

I looked around to see that the Treehouse was pretty far away, so I dumped high—about four grand. Bob must have gained a little altitude in the ordeal, and I was thankful because I needed it to get back to the target.

After opening, I proceeded to fly to the landing area. I landed and everybody was wondering why I was so far away on exit. I told the story as they helped me with my gear. Someone always took my gear when I landed, and then put on my banner. I went straight to the bathroom and collapsed on a toilet. I was crying in agony and thankful I had made it. Then I got myself together and limped straight to the nearest beer and chair.

Later, as was traditional, they called up the skydivers to present us with trophies. I limped up there and explained my ordeal to all the naked people. By now the back of my knee was black and blue and the bruise was about the size of a dinner plate. I proceeded to drink mass quantities and was doing what I could to smile through the pain.

I remembered Moorehead telling us that even if we break a leg on a demo, to get up and walk away smiling. Yes sir, Captain Pat.

Sandy Harper-Calliham

Get Out, Get Out, Get Out

In 1984 a group of us signed up for a balloon jump in Wildomar. We drove up very early from San Diego and I was surprised that at least 15 or 20 people showed up. With just one balloon, I wondered how we'd all get up before the winds came up.

My girlfriend Karen, me and a guy we'd never met before were on the second load so we took off with everyone making the usual corny Wizard of Oz jokes. I noticed the pilot was lying on the burner kind of hard, but figured he was in a hurry to get everyone up.

Then I started looking closely at the inside of the balloon envelope and noticed it certainly didn't look new; in fact, it looked kind of ratty overall. But, what did I know about balloons? Karen and I were getting to know our new friend and found out he had just a hundred jumps and was from Perris. He was kind of nervous, but that seemed normal for the number of jumps he had.

At 1,500 feet I heard a very strange noise and we all looked up. I was startled to see blue sky where I should have seen balloon. What happened was the pilot, in a hurry to get to altitude, was over-heating the envelope and the Velcro that held the top of the balloon in place had failed. That's the part you pull the rope on to release the hot air after landing (and oddly enough the part balloonists call the "parachute"). A bit more than half of it was detached.

And so, down we went.

I knew we had to get out. I already knew it, but the pilot was screaming, "Get out! You gotta get out now!" We were passing through about 1,300 feet when I said to Karen, "You need to go, honey. Do a good three seconds and throw the main. Then get out from under the balloon." And she did it perfectly.

I heard the pilot screaming into the radio about an in-flight emergency and the thought struck me: What are they going to do on the other end, send us a ladder? But then I realized he was probably thinking more about medical care after an emergency landing. He now had the burner going at full blast trying to salvage whatever lift we had left.

Now it was the other guy's turn. But he was freaking out. We were almost at a thousand feet and descending pretty quickly. I pleaded with him to jump and finally resorted to saying I'd leave him there, but nothing was working. I thought for a second of just throwing him over the side by force, but he didn't have an AAD (students, not experienced jumpers, used them regularly back then) so I couldn't bring myself to do that. Then I told him, "I'll hold your pilot chute. All you have to do is jump!" I reached down to grab his handle, but he pushed me away.

Meanwhile, through all this, the pilot is still screaming, "Get out, get out, get out!!!"

When we descended below a grand, I swear I could see the needle on my altimeter actually moving downward. I climbed up on the side of the basket and gave the guy one more chance by offering him my hand, but he was frozen solid. So I yelled one last thing at him, "If you decide to jump, don't hit me!" And I bailed out.

I did about a five-second delay, and when I felt I was going fast enough, dumped my main. I was under canopy at about 600 feet. I did two quick spirals to pick up some speed and flew out from under the balloon. Good thing I did, too. I saw something out of the corner of my eye; it was the other skydiver. He passed me about 100 feet away in freefall, on his back, kicking and flailing. I yelled, "Pull, dump, get something out!"

But he just kept going. I figured I was just about to see the dust ring from his impact when I saw one of his pilot chutes launch. He'd finally pulled his reserve and after a few seconds, he landed hard under his round reserve.

I landed, looked for Karen, and saw her standing some ways away, but now here comes the balloon. The envelope looked more like a streamering canopy than anything else, but the pilot still had the burner going when he crashed into the ground.

I ran over expecting the worse, but he was still alive. I remembered my lifesaving procedures from the Marine Corps and cleared his airway (all his teeth were broken.) He was bleeding from the legs with multiple compound fractures. I ripped my shirt off and held pressure on the worst of the leg wounds as best I could, and was thankful I could hear sirens in the distance. The chase truck was also now in sight. The pilot, thankfully, lived and made a full recovery.

About two months later I received a letter in the mail with the balloon company logo on it; inside was a check for $70. The pilot refunded both Karen's and my jump ticket. I thought that was pretty classy.

About a year later I was working at the DZ in Ramona when one morning, the balloon pilot showed up. He asked, "Hey Nick, can you teach me to jump?"

It seemed he was ready to start ballooning again but vowed never again without a parachute. I talked it over with Frank Mott, the DZO, and asked him if I could throw the guy a free first-jump course. Frank agreed. We talked about the incident that day and I asked him, "What do you think would have happened if we'd all been whuffos just going for a balloon ride, instead of jumpers?"

"With all that weight in the basket, we would have all died," he said.

He sat my static-line course and jumped a big round T-10. Frank sold him a pilot's rig and everyone lived happily ever after. Well, so far anyway.

Nick DiGiovanni

Great View of a Night Skydive

My harrowing story was at Perris, sometime during the late 1970s. Many of us who had been jumping with Steve Fielding at Elsinore had good night jump equipment that he made and sold—red or strobe lights mounted to boxes with batteries inside, activated with a handy toggle switch on the box. They were taped to the top backside of our helmets. Very cool. We turned them on right before exit.

Well, I never gave all this much thought until one jump where someone (a relatively new skydiver) had improvised a night light by taping a flashlight to the top of his helmet. Although it wasn't as cool as ours, it was the same principle … or so we thought.

Usual jump run, floaters out, lights on! 3-2-1-GO! I was base and the flashlight guy was pin (we were doing it the hard way to qualify for NSCR.) I looked up and saw a huge bright white light with a beam that would light up the airfield coming straight at me.

None of us on the load had noticed that the guy had mounted the flashlight facing forward instead of backward. Well, as the star built, this new guy watched as each jumper came into the star, and blinded everyone in the process. Apparently he was enjoying his great view of his first night skydive (which I believe also was his NSCR qualification jump.)

It was kind of funny to watch the facial reactions of everyone when they broke wrists and were suddenly in the spotlight. There were a lot of grimaces, shocked expressions, squeezed-shut eyes, sudden head turns, and useless shouting as everyone instantly lost their night vision.

Needless to say, we all had a lot of night jump advice for Perris's one and only Scott Smith (if my memory serves me right) when we finished that skydive!

Nancy Gruttman-Tyler

Focus, Focus, Focus

I was jumpmaster with three static-line students, and Debbie Blackmon's husband Brick was flying their C-182. We took off toward the lake at Elsinore, did a 180-degree turn, and were passing over the dairy east of the DZ at 1,500 feet when the engine threw a rod through the side of the engine case.

Oil completely covered the wind screen, but worse, the plane was vibrating so badly I thought the prop was coming off or the engine was trying to tear itself from its mounts.

Brick did a 180 back toward the DZ, which I wished he hadn't as we lost a good bit of altitude. I wasn't sure we'd make it without losing control, so I put out the first student on his reserve and then the other two.

I wasn't too sure about Brick's judgment. He was a commuter pilot for Skies West (we used to call it "Skies Worst".) One morning he was supposed to fly to Palm Springs to pick up a flight in his C-152. But the 152 wouldn't start. So he had hand-propped it by himself and it started, but he'd already untied one side of the plane and had the throttle in too far. It started with a roar, did a big circle and creamed into his other airplane, a 182, sitting right next to it. The big joke was "who do you know that wrecked two of his airplanes in one day?"

By the time I got the last student out, we were passing through 600 feet and still on the other side of Cereal Road; I knew we'd never make the runway (and I could see that Brick was way too focused on this goal.)

I always told student jumpers that the whole world is a drop zone and you only need enough room to land a canopy, and just don't hit anything. Fixating on making the DZ is what can kill you. It's the same with airplanes. Land under control, going as slow as you can, and you've got a good shot at not dying.

We were starting to stall as he was milking the glide, so I bailed out over the field with all the power lines and transformers in it. I hooked a low turn to find a clear patch. This was long before anyone was swooping, and I was amazed how fast my Cruiselite canopy skimmed across the ground and how far I went before I touched down. Runway rash … but no injuries.

Brick managed a safe but rough landing in the student landing area.

Nick DiGiovanni

Seemed Like A Good Idea at the Time

It began as a normal event at the DZ, but by the end it had become a NSTIWTIWGD moment.

One of our better pilots, Jim *"Flyin' W"* Wilkins, was goofing around before he landed, so Jerry Ryan and I decided to challenge him by holding a wind streamer stretched between us (anyone remember those things?) We wanted to see if he would swoop and cut it with the propeller.

He saw us and took the challenge. When he was about 200 feet away, I started to have second thoughts. Those yellow streamers were only about 12 to 15 feet long, and that C-182 (or was it a 206?) started looking really big.

Jim never wavered. He flew right at it and cut it just fine. The prop did not bother me so much, but I forgot that the wheels stuck out pretty far. That got my attention about .03 seconds before Jim cut the streamer.

It's amazing how short your life seems as it flashes before your eyes when you are young and dumb.

Tim Long

Cow Pie, Rattlesnake, What's The Difference?

Sometime in the mid-1980s (before audible altimeters) I was video-ing a four-way at Otay (Borderland). We didn't dirt dive; we just threw it together. The last point was a star, and in the video you can see that we somehow held the formation through two grand. You can see the first person leave the formation, then the next one right after—which was about 1,600 feet.

Now it's a two-way with Duffy Fainer and another guy. In the video, if you watch closely, you can see one guy—blonde hair, no helmet—do a double-take on his wrist-mount and dart away.

Now we were just above a grand, maybe 1,200 feet. I knew we were getting low, but I never looked at my altimeter since doing something sensible like that would have disrupted the continuity of the video. I was unaware of just how low we were. Then, like an idiot, I pointed to Duffy, indicating he should pull first so I could film his opening.

What you don't see in the video are two guys in their fishing boat at the eastern tip of Otay Lake, leaning back and looking straight up at me. I will never forget that sight. I swear I thought I was going to land right between them. I whipped out my main and prayed that there would be no pilot chute hesitation, because if it did hesitate, all three of us were about to die!

I estimate that I pulled at about 500 feet. It may have been higher; I don't know because I wasn't going to look at my altimeter then either!

Don Mumma saw Duffy's canopy open, but not mine. From his perspective, I was still in freefall when I disappeared behind a tree. He was so sure that I had bounced on the other side of the lake that he called the San Diego County Coroner.

It took me an hour and a half in the hot, late-Spring sun to get to a point where I could safely walk across the lake. Eventually I arrived at the point where the jump planes taxi out—where the beginning of the runway starts—at the far eastern end of the DZ. All I had to do was walk across the narrow stream and I was home free. No big deal.

But as I stood there taking off my shoes, I heard a noise behind me, behind the berm. I couldn't see it, but it was a familiar sound—a Cessna 180 was about to land and was headed right at me. I dove into the wet and muddy ground, barely missing the landing gear as it screamed over me and touched down just on the other side of the stream.

Now I was pissed—after getting dirty and wet on top of being hot, exhausted, and very thirsty. But here came a 180 taxiing out with a load of jumpers. As it rotated to takeoff position, I saw one jumper through the open door, sitting with his back against the instrument panel. He mouthed the words, "You're alive." I almost lost it.

The next thing I saw was Duffy and several others sprinting over to me. There had been a wagon riding the back hills looking for me—it was the coroner. Everyone was pleased that they didn't have to shut down the DZ because I impacted off-site.

As Duffy and I strategized about how to get me across the little stream, I was reminded that rattlesnakes love to sun themselves in the Spring. I even mentioned that I was concerned about this. Now that I've cheated death twice, I told Duffy, I would follow his footsteps exactly so as to avoid any unpleasant poisonous creatures with my bare feet.

Of course, he stepped on what looked like a cow pie, but as my left foot came down, the pie suddenly came alive, lifted its head, and stuck its little forked tongue out at me. It was a baby rattler, and my next step would have been into its waiting mouth.

Randy Forbes

No Shit There I Was, Skygods All Around Me

There was an announcement over the PA system at Elsinore. It was Al Krueger and his Sky Pirates telling everyone who wanted to jump with them to write their name on a paper and put it in a hat. Well, I ran up there and tossed in my name. Thinking nothing more, I went back to packing.

Then I heard my name, and I'm dreaming! Me...jump with them? I don't have my logbook handy so I don't remember everyone who was on the jump, but Al and Chuck Anderson briefed me before we went up. They said they usually hooked their hooks together and whatever I did, I wasn't to break wrist on the hooks. I was so damn excited, that was the longest climb to altitude I've ever experienced.

I think they put me out in the middle of the 10-way. Five left and cut...we're out the door. They built it pretty fast below me. I had a habit of getting there too fast and going low, so was hanging out and above.

On my approach I remembered what Al and Chuck had said, i.e., don't close between us. But as I made my move and was coming in, the star turned a little. I'm there and right in front of me is my slot. Yep, Al and Chuck locked together.

I was not going to pass up this opportunity, so I grabbed each hook and literally had to pry them apart. Suddenly Chuck's hook hit me smack dab in the nose. Thought I was going to die (well, sort of)...if not from blood-letting, then Chuck or Al would kill me when I landed.

Blood was in front of me and on my goggles. Did I care? Hell no, I was jumping with the Skygods! I saw smiles all around and Chuck had a weird look on his face.

We broke off and I was screaming under canopy. Not realizing that they might think I was hurt (because of the blood all over my face) I continued to scream in absolute excitement.

When I landed, the cheers began in the target area. I told them I was okay. Al and Chuck congratulated me and were amazed at my determination. We got back to the packing area and I was as buzzed as a rabbit on speed. Purple Patty walked up to me and suggested that I wash my face because there was blood all over it...like I really cared. Well, in the bathroom I realized my nose was a little off to the side and was really starting to swell and hurt.

I was taken to the ER, where the doctors quickly diagnosed me with a broken nose. I think I had about 75 jumps and when I went back over to Perris, I was now a Skygod (with a black eye and a broken nose.)

I heard that breaking into a formation between Al and Chuck had only been done a couple of times, and there was a patch for it. Never got the patch, but there I was and I thought I was gonna die…but what a way to go.

Sandy Harper-Calliham

I Hope Nobody Saw That

I'll tell a story I witnessed from the ground.

Early in the days of the Paradactyl, they used a reefing line with a pin to slow down its deployment. The chute opened about halfway; releasing the pin opened it all the way. That pin had a line down to the risers that needed to be pulled out after the opening. If it opened with line twists (and being a triangular canopy, it almost always did) the pin wouldn't come out. You had to twist your body around to unwind the lines in order to get the pin released.

There was a gentleman jumping at Elsinore named Art Shehan; he wore very thick glasses. We watched him under canopy from the packing tables as he tried to release the pin—all the way down to 500 feet. He couldn't get the pin released, and to our amazement he then cut away.

Since he was leaning backwards trying to release the pin when he chopped it, he went into a perfect back loop. He leveled out before dumping the reserve as we were all taught to do. He was probably at 200 to 300 feet at that point—but luckily, at sub-terminal speed.

The reserve opened and didn't even breathe once before he was on the ground. He told us later that he got up, brushed off the dust, and thought, *"I hope nobody saw that."*

Little did he know that we had all watched it. Somebody had a very early video camera with a long lens on it and videotaped the whole thing. We watched that tape over and over again. We joked that with his thick glasses, he was able to visually calculate his altitude to the last inch.

John Jennings

Flying Backwards, PLF, Explosion

My last jump was on May 20, 1979. It was a demo that I had organized for my new whuffo boyfriend's nephew. They were having their 4th annual May Fest picnic, and he just happened to run the idea by me. Of course, I said yes. I hadn't jumped in a month, so I was ready.

I went to the DZ to see who would jump with me. Mike Owens, Tim Long and Sally Wenner rounded out the load. It was a cloudy day, and Mike was wearing smoke.

Okay, we're over the target and we have low clouds. We bailed out at two grand, and I had a pilot chute hesitation. I punched my backpack with my right elbow, and off she went.

Tim, Mike and Sally followed me out. I looked around and saw three good chutes and Mike's smoke dangling, so all was well.

But not for me. I looked up and was a bit confused for a second. My square was fully open but something wasn't quite right. Oh god, the "effin" thing was flying backwards! I was over the crowd and in a good place to set up for the landing site where the ground crew was waiting for us. But I was kind of in a panic, as I was having a hard time trying to figure out how to steer backwards.

All the while I could hear Bob laughing his ass off yelling, "Over here, Sandy, over here."

No Shit, Bob...I knew where you were; I just couldn't figure out how to get there.

I realized I wasn't going to land at the target. My next thought was *okay, how am I going to miss all the cars?*...because that's where I was headed. Meanwhile, I heard fire engines because the field was on fire where Mike had dropped his smoke grenade.

Now I was headed for a van with windows on the side. I looked over my shoulder, thinking *"I'm not going to slam into those windows!"*

So I grabbed a riser, turned to miss the van, and slammed into the trunk of the car behind it. I landed feet first and did the most hellacious PLF off that trunk that you ever saw. My knees were up in my chin, and I was surprised I didn't snap my bum leg.

My boyfriend came running over and helped me up. My legs were shaking, but I stood up. I walked over to the target, where I found Tim, Sally and Mike. We went to the microphone to introduce ourselves, but the mike had just been turned off. I had some pain in my legs, but I figured I could medicate with some beer.

Then I heard a loud boom and saw fire and smoke. The fire department was still there and it was a good thing, because the car I landed on had several gallons of gas stored in its trunk. After I collided with it, the fumes and heat in the closed trunk had exploded. I could have been blown up.

The owner of the car had been looking for me and the fire department was looking for him. He didn't find me, but they found him and gave him several tickets.

I put all my gear in my kit bag and it has been there for more than 31 years.

Sandy Harper-Calliham

Special Occasions Only

It was an eight-way demo jump in 1973 over Jackson Northside High School, and my 267th jump. We flew the Beech over from Covington, Tenn. I was the only jumper with smoke.

I exited first, the formation built successfully, I began to track, waved off and deployed, opening at 2,500 feet, but with line twists. I kicked out of the twists, reached for the toggles, and saw Greg Giles under canopy impact my canopy, causing a partial collapse.

Training, fear and adrenaline kicked in to produce the following verbal command: "See ya!!"

I cut away, rolled on my back to wave at Greg, and deployed my reserve from a belly-mounted pop-top low-profile reserve container. I was slightly head down on deployment, however, and I observed it burbling between my feet.

Then the pilot chute bounced off the smoke bracket. NSTIWTIWGD!

My reserve deployed at just under 2,000 feet and I landed near the crowd.

Whuffo: "Wow, that smoke and double parachute stunt was cool!"
Me: "Yeah, we do that for special occasions only!"

Larry Frankenbach

Unconscious and Falling

In Texas on December 22, 1966, 16 expert parachutists met at a small pasture five miles from the Gulf of Mexico between Galveston and Houston. After two weeks of planning, they were ready to attempt free fall jumps from the edge of space.

At 12:15 that afternoon, the first five loaded their jump aircraft: a 206 Super Cessna Skywagon. It roared down the narrow grass runway and climbed upward into the 21-below-zero temperature at 25,000 feet, into air so thin it robs a man of useful consciousness in minutes by oxygen starvation, or hypoxia as the doctors call it. They were climbing into trouble.

We were manifested for the second lift to 25,000 feet. So, as the plane took off, we watched with more than casual interest. Tim, an ex-jet fighter pilot who had lost his left eye flying for the Marines, turned to me with a grin and a shrug, "Well, they made it off the ground, but I'll lay you odds that one of those clowns screws up before they even leave the airplane."

Some 37 minutes later, when the Cessna reached jump altitude, the thin air and cold had done their deadly work. Only two of the five skydivers aboard were able to jump. One of the others had been so affected by the cold, or his nerves, that he froze in the door and did not jump; another had accidentally unhooked his oxygen line so that when it came time to jump he was only able to turn blue and babble. During the ascent he had been sucking on an oxygen line that wasn't connected to the oxygen tank and as a result, the necessary state of mental alertness was replaced by confusion and euphoria.

The third jumper had suffered the consequences of gas expansion which occurs at high altitudes. When he was carried from the aircraft on the ground, I solicitously removed his lined jump suit and carefully scraped the frozen vomit from it. Warmer than mine, I wanted to use it for my upcoming jump. Little did I realize that before the day ended I, too, would be lying unconscious at 25,000 feet far out over the chilly waters of the Gulf of Mexico in a plane piloted by a man whose oxygen-starved brain convinced him that north was best reached by flying south.

The two that did jump grossly misjudged their exit point so that they landed some five miles away. Although we blamed it on stupidity at the time, later events indicated that their misjudgment was caused by the insidious dullness which accompanies hypoxia. Just what is hypoxia?

Hypoxia means not enough oxygen in the bloodstream. It is a silent killer, as the symptoms are seldom unpleasant and there is no pain. The accompanying impairment of muscle coordination and judgment is not noticed by the pilot or jumper. In effect, you can suffocate without ever being aware of it.

In the thin air of 18,000 feet, you can breathe less than half as many molecules of oxygen into your lungs as you can with each breath at sea level. As a result, your body undergoes rapid and severe psychological and physical changes. You experience headaches, light-headedness, marked fatigue, labored respiration and mental impairment: you just can't react or perform in a normal manner. Collapse is imminent. At 23,000 feet, 8 to 15 minutes of exposure leads to convulsions, cessation of respiration and circulation, and death.

The onset of hypoxia could cause a pilot suffering from its effects to fly straight into a mountain without blinking. He feels exhilarated and weak at the same time; he may see the mountain and know it is there without being able to do a thing to miss it, or care.

Some people maintain that they can hold their breath for two or three minutes. This, they feel, should give them a longer time of useful consciousness in the event of oxygen failure. What they fail to understand is that your whole body needs oxygen to survive, not just your lungs. The human body is porous so that even a saturated system of oxygen will rapidly diminish and induce cellular damage in the brain, leaving you a babbling idiot.

To avoid the devastating effects of oxygen starvation, all aircraft which operate at altitudes over 12,000 feet must supply supplementary oxygen to the pilot and passengers. Big commercial airliners pressurize their cabins to an oxygen content of 4,000 feet to avoid having an oxygen mask for each passenger.

On light aircraft, however, such as our Cessna 206, 100 percent pure aviation oxygen is carried in a tank. When the plane reaches 12,000 feet, passengers and pilots simply plug their individual oxygen masks into this central tank and hypoxia is avoided.

To us jumpers on the ground the possibility of hypoxia seemed remote. We were more worried about the cold.

The sun shone through broken clouds and above their scattered whiteness, the sky was clear all the way up to 12,000 feet where a light layer of broken cirrus clouds seemed to divide the sky. Below these clouds is most of the air we breathe: 90 percent of the earth's oxygen. Above is nothing except dark blue sky and cold.

The temperature drops ten degrees for every thousand feet you climb. Above the clouds the air is too thin to retain any of the sun's heat. On the day we made our ill-fated jump, the temperature was 21 degrees below zero at 25,000 feet. And the wind-chill effect at that altitude makes the cold even more deadly.

Like most jump craft, the twin waist cargo doors of our Cessna had been removed, creating a large opening 2-1/2 feet wide by 39 inches high, for easy in-flight exits. This leaves a gaping hole in the side of the airplane which acts as a funnel for cold air. Air so cold it will freeze a gloved hand in minutes.

But we were confident that we would be in complete control of any situation which might arise. We didn't expect to be at that altitude long enough to encounter any danger. We were grossly overconfident.

Our aircraft was a good one. The 1966 Turbocharged 206 Cessna Super Skywagon has plenty of horsepower, even in the thin air of 20,000 feet where the rate of climb is 500 to 700 feet-per-minute.

The average round trip to and from 25,000 feet is 45 minutes. Our trip was to take over two hours.

To take care of the oxygen requirements of the pilot and passengers, this Cessna has a tank behind the baggage space. A pressure gauge is located on the bulkhead and is easily visible for in-flight reference. Overhead, above the windows, each passenger has a female receptacle to accommodate the plug on his oxygen mask hose. Masks are simple rebreather types held to the head with an elastic band. Unfortunately, all of the masks in our aircraft were either broken off or removed from the oxygen line, leaving the jumper with a bare hose to stick in his mouth and suck on. Each individual system has a small spring-loaded check valve in the clear plastic oxygen hose. When oxygen is flowing, the valve is held open.

Thirty minutes after the Cessna returned to the ground, we were rigged up, loaded and ready to go. As the wheels lifted off, I tried unsuccessfully to adjust my position so that the coming cold would not blow directly across my body. In the back of the plane, Tim sat and fiddled with his oxygen line. Beside him sat Don, inscrutable in a cold-weather mask and dark glasses. Ed, a 23-year-old dental student from Houston, was sitting in the door. He was to act as jumpmaster and pick the spot over which we would exit. His choice of an exit point would determine where we landed.

In the front, next to the pilot, sat Skippy, a field engineer for a construction firm in Houston. Skippy, a short and muscular fellow, had been a pro boxer in his youth. I was sitting on one side of the open door, facing Ed.

As the plane climbed we tried to assure ourselves that our jump would go better than the jump which had preceded. We decided to keep up a rapid cross-talk so that anyone suffering from the altitude would be quickly noticed by his friends even if he himself was oblivious to his condition. In addition, we assigned partners. Each man would have someone to look after. We weren't going to make the mistakes that the first load had made. My partner was Ed and I was to look after Skippy.

Some 20 minutes after takeoff, at about 12,000 feet, it began to get cold. Plans were forgotten as we attempted to assure that we would not be too cold to move when the time came to exit. My face went completely numb.

At 16,000 feet we hooked up to the oxygen supply. With the tubes stuck in our mouths, conversation was difficult; later it would be impossible.

It took me several minutes to get accustomed to breathing through a thin tube. I let the oxygen trickle into my mouth until my cheeks were puffed out with the pure oxygen, and then I'd breathe in. As I looked around, everyone seemed to be having the same difficulty. Except for the pilot. Having been up to 25,000 feet once that day, he apparently felt that he was an old pro and didn't hook up till the plane reached 18,000 feet.

From 18,000 ft. the ground looks strange and unreal. Most of the color which you would expect to see is replaced by a cold gray. Thin clouds that looked like wisps of ice made things seem even more unreal.

At 20,000 feet, the wind rushing into the cabin has a different sound—a higher pitched whistle instead of the usual roar. The lower pressure and thinness of the atmosphere gave me an airy, bloated feeling. Climbing at over 1,000 feet per minute, the Cessna reached altitude in just under 40 minutes. However, we remained at that altitude for over one hour.

The temperature was well below zero. The cold whipped in the open door, driven by the 175-mph speed of the aircraft. My legs grew numb. The five of us sat and sucked on the oxygen lines as if they contained pure ambrosia.

My altimeter still showed 20,000 feet, but it hadn't been working properly lately. Anyway, as long as I could see the ground in freefall, the trees rushing up would paint a graphic picture of my altitude and tell me when to pull my ripcord. If you have to depend entirely on your altimeter to tell you how high you are above the ground and when to pull, you are likely to dig yourself a hole on impact if something goes wrong.

The plane turned onto jump run, Ed threw off his blanket, nodded to us and began to sight along the edge of the door to the drop zone far below. Still sucking on his tube of oxygen, he made thumb motions to Skippy up front who relayed the direction of turn to the pilot. Looking over Ed's shoulder I could see the target area: four miles down, a bit ahead and to the right.

One small ten-degree turn and two minutes more and we would be directly over our exit point. Excitement began to build. Just two more minutes.

I got on my knees to unhook my oxygen, and then passed it up front for Skippy to stow out of the windblast. As I awaited Ed's command to exit, dizziness came over me like a cold fever. My head throbbed and my stomach turned. Ed made circular motions with his hand to the left; my head moved with his hand. The two minutes had passed and despite his repeated requests for a ten-degree left turn, we had continued straight ahead and up, missing the exit point by over a mile.

Ed wanted another pass; I wanted some oxygen. Still, instead of a hard bank and a quick pass we began a slow sweep to the right, out over the Gulf of Mexico. I suddenly lost all of my energy. I knew I needed some oxygen, and quick.

Others had their problems, too. When Ed shifted in the door to spot, Tim slid over to watch and double check. He braced his hand on the open doorsill where it froze almost immediately. Meanwhile, thinking that we would soon be around for another jump run, I borrowed "drags" of oxygen from Don and Ed and waited for the plane to turn.

But for some reason the pilot refused to turn the aircraft. He sat hunched over the controls, dark glasses, his parka, and oxygen mask shielding his face. He hadn't hooked up his oxygen until 18,000 feet and was now floating in the mental confusion of hypoxia. He probably understood what the signals meant, but couldn't relate them to turning the aircraft. We were at 25,000 feet. Unable to figure out why Ed was wasting time, Skippy pushed back to the door: "What the goddamn hell is going on? Let's go!"

Wordlessly Ed pointed down to the gray waters of the Gulf of Mexico, then out to the receding coastline of Texas. Skippy took one look and returned up front to convince the pilot to turn. I had a strange floaty kind of feeling; somehow I felt more like a spectator than a participant in this crazy game of getting the aircraft back over land.

I watched nature unfold a panorama of conditions at 25,000 feet. The most noticeable thing was the ice. With the onset of hypoxia the cold had ceased to bother me. But ice was everywhere. My chest and lap were covered with a light frost of moisture frozen out of my breath. All of the metal fittings on my chute and boots had grown snowy beards of frost. Ed had icicles frozen on his chin from his running nose. It was like the winter scenes in *"Dr. Zhivago."*

Around us the thin air seemed to turn darker. Below, the waters of the Gulf were an unpleasant black, spotted by soft cotton puffs of clouds.

Inside appeared even more unreal. Don sat blue-lipped and silent, sucking on an oxygen tube with the intense concentration of a hash smoker seeking release. He held the frozen hand of Tim who was now curled on the floor crying words I couldn't understand. The inside of the cabin was done in a soft yellow fabric, fuzzy like a blanket. The instrument panel was the only thing alive, it seemed. Its gauges registered four hundred feet of climb per minute and a slow motion bank to the left. The cold surrounded me.

Oxygen—who ever misses it? Here I was dying without it. Man, what a gas. I had to get some air, and soon, but Skippy was arguing with the pilot and I couldn't break in to convince them to give me my mask. Besides, I didn't have enough wind to whistle, much less shout. Tim was still curled up in a tight ball. His shaking was causing the wing tips to quiver in harmony. Ed was still trying to get the plane turned, and Skippy had quit talking and was pounding the pilot on the back and shoulder. It was like an old-time movie.

Don gave me a drag from his tube and I lay down and shut my eyes. I was unable to think sitting up. Slapping me, Don peered closely into my face. He stuck his oxygen in my mouth while he tried to get someone up front to pass my mask back to me.

Shaking so hard he could hardly talk, Tim addressed the world in general: "I'm freezing; really, I'm freezing … I can't take much more … I'm goddamn freezing to death. We have got to go out or down … I don't care which … I'm freezing."

We turned, but in a circle.

By then I couldn't care less. Don handed me my oxygen equipment. As I fumbled with the tubing which had become stiff with the cold, the plane began to return to course. Unable to hook up the oxygen with my numb hands, it seemed like a good idea in my addled brain to remove my gloves. Working in slow motion, I finally got the line plugged in and secured.

Then came the problem of putting my gloves back on. It just couldn't be done. I didn't have enough coordination to clap my hands together. I knew that I wanted to put them on, but couldn't figure out how to make my hands obey the commands of my brain. The effort was making me dizzy. My fingernails were blue, which struck me as funny. Attempting a stern frame of mind, I tried to will my hands to work. I got my gloves on only to discover that I couldn't feel them. Further, the exercise had worn me out so I laid back down, thinking that perhaps if I didn't move I could resupply my blood with the needed oxygen.

Meanwhile, Ed and Skippy somehow got us pointed toward the drop zone. I don't remember much of what went on. I do remember my altimeter swinging wildly from 22,000 to 25,000 ft., with the intermittent buzzing of the plane's stall indicator warning device for punctuation.

Suddenly Ed unplugged his oxygen and said, "Jump run." Tim seemed to come out of shock. Don unplugged and turned to me, "Are you OK?"

"Yeah. Be glad to get some air ..."

"You sure you're OK now?"

"Yes ... Hell yes, if you think I'm going to stay in this plane, you're crazy."

We unhooked and waited. The nightmare repeated itself. The pilot refused or couldn't make the final corrections necessary for us to reach the drop zone. We needed still another turn.

When we realized we couldn't jump yet, we spent the next several moments hooking up life-giving oxygen lines with clumsy hands. By now we were all suffering from the cold and lack of oxygen. But for some un-fathomable reason, no one considered going back down.

Except Tim. His frozen hand had thawed enough to really hurt. In addition, he was getting the full force of the freezing wind across his body. There was an expression of hurt on his face that was total and complete. He leaned toward Don and spoke a voice that wavered for control. "I'm hurting bad. I think my hand is frozen. You've got to convince them that I'm hurt." His voice broke. "Make them understand ... I'm hurt ... We've got to get out or go down ..."

Don didn't reply. He held Tim's frozen hand between his own and kept nodding his head, like a mechanical Santa in a store window.

Finally hooked up, we all sat immobile, content just to be still and breathe. Then, in a rushing panic, the implications of our inaction hit me. Pulling off my mask I began to pound on the pilot's back and scream, "Turn this sonofabitching airplane around! Turn around ... !"

Don grabbed my fist and said crisply, "Shut up." The pilot didn't even glance around.

Dizzy from exertion and somewhat ashamed, I tried to explain, "Tim's right; we've got to go out or get down to air."

Punctuating his speech with sips of oxygen, Don replied, "Next pass—we either go out—or take the plane down."

His eyeglass frames covered with frost, Ed spoke for the first time. He had removed his oxygen mask and stuck the tubing down his throat so that, with the bone whiteness of his frozen face, he resembled a hospital patient who wasn't going to make it. "What the hell; we've made it this far—let's go one more pass—then jump."

No reply was made or expected, so we each turned back to our own problems. Skippy and Ed worked in a team to get the airplane back around over the field. Skippy would relay Ed's hand instructions to the pilot and prod him into carrying them out. Completely absorbed with pain, Tim sat and shivered convulsively while Don sat like a mother hen over the two of us. I had returned to my prone eyes-shut position to wait. The time had to come when we would exit—get out in freefall where there was plenty of air.

My mind began to wander crazily: Don't trust airplanes. All you need is some air and a parachute and zingo, you're an airplane. Boy, from this high—just like a jet airplane—whoosh, with clouds hitting you in the face. Clouds? Now is the time for all good men to come to the aid of their country and fellow man.

With a silly smile, I opened my eyes and stared at Skippy who was slapping me in the face. He had stuffed the mouthpiece of his oxygen bag into his mouth. The bag expanded and contracted with his breathing like an extra lung. There was ice in the bottom of the bag. He said to Don, "Should we let him jump?" Don shrugged; I smiled. Come hell or high water, I am going to jump.

"Jump run," but nobody moved to disconnect their oxygen. I taxied to the door and prepared to take off, still happily sucking at my oxygen. Ed yelled "Cut!" … the engine slowed, and the roar of the wind abated.

Ed hopped out into the blinding sky. I spit out my oxygen and took off after him—only to be caught by an iron fist of cold and flung tumbling. A slow roll on my back silhouetted the airplane which perversely seemed to be falling up, white oxygen masks streaming in the wind. Grabbing air, I arched and stabled out, excitement rushing through my veins like ice water.

Outstretched on the air, the other jumpers floated. Hands at sides, I dipped my head and air roared by as I dove down to them. They loomed up like overstuffed man-birds, all wearing intense grins. Skippy sailed past, his boots covered with frost. I turned and followed him. He turned to face me and we slid together for a perfect two-man hook-up. My altimeter read 18,000 feet. Another 16,000 feet to go til pull time.

A wave of uncomfortable lassitude came over me. With mild curiosity I watched the rim of the world below go dark and narrow around me. The dark slowly closed in, leaving a large-ish spot of vision that rapidly grew smaller. It was as if I were falling into a black funnel toward the small end which was snapping shut in front of me.

Just before I went totally unconscious, my mind unvoiced the realization of the "tunnel vision" phenomenon. There was nothing I could do. I passed out exactly when the tunnel snapped shut, at about 7,000 feet, I guess.

How much time goes by while you are unconscious? I aroused slowly, knowing I was skydiving, unconcerned about having just awakened from oblivion. I knew that something was wrong. Unable to focus on the particulars, I began a systems check.

I couldn't see my altimeter. In fact, nothing was visible except a diffuse bright glow. It was like looking at the sun through clouds. Was I falling on my back looking up at the clouds? If so, then I was falling upward because the light was getting brighter! What could cause this to happen? Hmmmm, I can't relate to what is happening.

I pulled my ripcord chanting, "When in doubt, whip it out." Opening shock saddled me into the parachute harness and a sharp pain, unnoticed before this, washed over me so that I cried out.

My head ... no, my eardrums, were exploding. I still couldn't see. I tore off my goggles and the suddenly visible ground was right below me. I was open over a Texas pasture. The grass was yellow and dry under the warm sun. It was the feeble reflection of the sun off this grass that I'd seen through my frozen goggles. It got brighter as I rushed toward it in freefall. My overwhelming feeling was pain in my eardrums. I let my arms drop to let observers on the ground know I was hurt, steering only enough to soften my landing.

Touchdown brought a blinding flash of pain to each part of my body that touched the ground ... feet, then knees and hands. My hands burned. And my legs tingled. Too stiff to rise. Too pained to think. My hands were too cold to remove my helmet. My eardrums and Eustachian tubes hurt badly. I stayed on my hands and knees, moaning and shifting my weight from hand to hand as the ground crew rushed up.

My hands eventually thawed out and I finally got warm. The tremendous change in air pressure from twenty-five thousand feet down to below one thousand feet in just over two minutes of freefall had put painful pressure on my eardrums. The hooded parka I wore under my helmet had sealed off my ears so that the pressures couldn't equalize. When it finally did, days later, the return of full hearing startled me with its volume. I spit up small amounts of blood from whatever had ruptured for several days. Since that day, I've been unable to SCUBA dive due to the ear problems.

Tim developed painful frostbite in his right hand. Skin peeled off his hand in sheets. His glass eye had frozen, frostbiting his eyelid. Don developed stomach cramps. While Ed didn't feel well for days, he and the other two had no serious problems.

The hazards of high-altitude jumps are serious enough that the United States Parachute Association has promulgated regulations to help ensure greater safety for participants. Experience in a high-altitude simulator pressure chamber is a must.

We thought we could handle it. We couldn't.

Pat Works

Sure, You Can Call It an Emergency

All through the late 1970s and early '80s I worked as an aircraft mechanic. I was at Oceanside Airport working for an outfit called Aero Pacific; we were rebuilding and refurbishing Helio Couriers and Helio Stallions. I know they sound like helicopters, but they were actually fixed wing STOL aircraft that were used mostly in Vietnam.

Anyway, we'd just outfitted new turbo chargers on one particular Helio Courier and we needed to test it. I grabbed the two Strong pilot rigs we had in the shop which (being a rigger and jumper) I had packed and maintained, along with a bottle of oxygen, and up we went to 20,000 feet.

I was in the right seat and we were directly over the airport at about 19,000 ft. when an oil line failed. We shut down the engine and started a nice controlled spin back down to the airport. I glanced out the window and noticed how really high up we were. I thought, *what the hell,* looked at my boss and said, "Hey, this is a sort of an emergency, right?"

It really wasn't; we were fine. But he nodded so I said, "I'm going to jump."

I had no altimeter but had made probably 50 bandit jumps over the years at Oceanside, so I took a couple of good sucks on the oxygen bottle, pushed open the door, and got out. I'd never jumped from that kind of high altitude.

After about 10 seconds I decided it was way too frigging cold, so I rolled over on my back and did a few practice pulls. When I flipped back over I'd been in freefall for what I thought was a very long time, but how high was I? I didn't know but I was still way too high to pull.

When I felt the air getting warmer and things started looking more normal, I got as big as I could and pulled the ripcord as close to two grand as I could. I didn't want to blow up the only canopy I had, nor get blown away from the airport under a round. I landed right next to the hangars.

Nick DiGiovanni

10-Way Bounce

I was at Elsinore on a cloudy day. The clouds had come in and out all day, and we decided to go for it. Maybe we'd find a hole above the DZ once we got to altitude. We decided to go for a 10-way round. Our pilot was Terry Stronks, and he was taking us up to 12,500 feet.

I was in the door going pin, and also spotting. Suddenly we were in a black cloud. I was talking, and wasn't sure where we were. We hadn't been climbing very long. Everyone was yelling that we should get out, but I was in the door looking down and all I saw was black. I also saw the wing waving like it was made out of rubber. The plane was making horrible sounds, and I swear I thought it was going to fall apart.

Not a good situation. Skydivers were pushing on me yelling, "Go, Sandy, Go..." I was yelling back, "No. I don't know where we are. I can't see the ground."

My arms were on both sides of the door now and everybody was standing, ready to push me out. I was a human shield; I turned around and screamed, "Calm the fuck down, everyone."

They backed off a bit. My altimeter was doing weird shit; I didn't trust it. Were we in some sort of vortex? All I could see was complete darkness in and out of the plane.

Then as quickly as it started, it was over. That black cloud had tried to chew us up and spit us out, but by that time we were flying fine. I looked out the door and realized we were over the Ortegas by only a few hundred feet.

That was a close one. We all finally realized how disastrous it would have been had I jumped and everyone followed me out the door. Terry screamed from the cockpit. He knew, too.

Finally we all settled down for the rest of the ride to altitude. Everyone then began thanking me for not jumping. That would have been the worst kind of 10-way—a 10-way bounce. I couldn't even imagine the headlines. Terry said he was ready to go, but knew he couldn't get past us. When the pilot is freaked out, you know it's serious.

When we did get to altitude, I remember telling everyone, "Okay, now we can jump." I don't even remember what we did in freefall. We were all still sort of shocked over the climb-out.

I gained a little respect that day. I wasn't on any mega loads, but after that day it didn't matter. I became an honorary spotter.

Sandy Harper-Calliham

Out-of-Body

One day when I got to the drop zone, I realized that I had forgotten my jumpsuit. Rob Thundercloud said he had an extra one that he would let me use. He and I went up to do a two-way just for fun, just to get our knees in the breeze.

On the way to altitude Rob told me that he had a strange dream where he had killed himself. Only it was with a twist. It was not by putting a gun to his head, but by another person who resembled him who was doing him in. Of course, I thought it was a silly dream, but he told me that in his culture it is an omen. It means something bad was about to happen. Clearly, he was worried.

Anyway, the two-way was uneventful and we were both just having fun in freefall. I hadn't jumped with Rob in a while, and I was thinking what a great skydive we were having. As I tracked away Rob decided to follow me, unbeknown to me. I had been jumping a Wizard that took a long time to open. So Rob pulled when I did, thinking we would have plenty of vertical separation as his canopy would open much sooner than mine.

What Rob didn't know was that I had a new canopy that opened much faster than my Wizard. I got opening shock, spun around, and was heading face-to-face toward Rob. I was a little above him and just before the collision I raised my legs and went through his suspension lines just above the slider and stopped.

I made it through. But we started spinning and I yelled, "Rob, I am going to cut away."

He answered: "Wait!" and I said "Okay" although I didn't understand why I had to wait. When he was ready he told me to chop it. I did. His canopy was malfunctioning, too, so a few seconds later, he also cut away.

After we landed, we both went to the Bomb Shelter and got a beer.

By the way, remember the beginning of this story when Rob told me about him killing himself by an out-of-body person? Guess who he saw when I was coming at him wearing his jumpsuit?

Bob Celaya

My Pucker Factor Did Come to the Surface

It was at Perris in 1976 or '77. The cloud cover was low; we didn't have enough altitude to do decent RW. It was my first "torpedo run" with Jim *"Flyin' W"* Wilkins at the controls of the Twin Beech.

I was told the pilot would fly as high as possible under the clouds and have the plane going full blast. We would be given the sign to get up, line up, and prepare to jump out with no engine cut. I was still new to the sport, and thought it'd be great fun.

I was told I'd be unstable for a while, to enjoy it, and then pull and have fun on the canopy ride down. Well, I was prepared for everything except when I was told to get up. I was glued to the floor; my gear weighed 100 pounds, and frustration was rampant. The plane was kind of in a dive—so, of course, fellow jumpers helped me get up.

I had never jumped out with full prop blast, and that was another surprise. I was totally unstable; the first time that had ever happened. All through student status I never was unstable.

Anyway, for a split second I felt like I was losing it but then as I descended, stability returned. It might sound like no big deal, but I remember the feeling of "no control" … which was foreign to me. I ended up loving torpedo runs—just something to do when playing hacky sack got old.

This is not exactly a very hairy "No Shit" story, but my pucker factor did come to the surface.

Mary Stage

Hey Man, No Brakes

This is a NSTIWTIGD skydiving story that happened completely on the ground. After a hard day's jumping, we were riding on Pat Conatser's yellow, loud-exhaust-noise (the muffler fell off and didn't get replaced so it sounded like a good ol' hot rod) toilet trolley that he used to pick up jumpers.

It was nighttime and we were playing hide and seek from Ben. We went up and down the runway several times, like an airplane trying to get airborne, trading turns driving and making all that noise, laughing and having a good time as usual.

Then we saw Ben's little truck headlights coming from the house (that they had just moved into) toward us. We drove to the far east side of the DZ, and shut off the motor so he would not hear or see us.

Ben drove up and down the runway, turning to shine his lights all around the area and DZ, but didn't find us. He went back up to the house. We waited for a while, boasting how great we were, started the trolley's engine, and did it all over again.

On the last good ride we had to jump off and push it to start, because all of the start and stopping of the engine had caused the battery to run down. Mike Duran jumped into the driver's (pilot's) seat, drove to the north end of the runway, turned around to line up on the center line, popped the clutch and off we went, hooting and hollering, looking to the right just before manifest to see if any lights were coming our way from the house, picking up speed, going faster and faster.

We got about halfway down the runway, going about as fast as the toilet trolley would go, really having a good time before finally realizing that the brakes were not at their best. I started to yell, "Hey man, no brakes" and more riders began yelling, "Hey man, no brakes, man."

Mike let off the gas, trying to stop that beautiful DZ pick-up machine (which Pat loved to flush) as we were flying down the runway, slowing some as we ran out of tarmac.

We realized that we were not going to stop in time, and we also realized that this was going to be one hell of a ride into the canal. We discussed what the best thing to do would be, i.e. ride it into the canal or bail.

Just before the end of the runway, Mike turned slightly to the left. I think most of us bailed; the others rode it into the water. As it bumped and banged down the side, I could hear yelling—lots of yelling.

Miraculously no one got hurt, but the trolley's toilet broke off and into several pieces. Pat was disappointed and Ben was pissed at me on general principles, but as far as I know, no one ever told what really happened.

Jim "Flyin' W" Wilkins

Is DDE Still Alive?

In September 1973, Dave Snyder arranged for a few of us to jump at an airshow in Abilene, Kansas. I had about 60 jumps. The airport was on the edge of town next to the railroad track, and right south of the Eisenhower Memorial where the former President is buried.

The wind was coming up and blew hard all day, but I got on a load with John Schuman, Clyde Godding and Cindy Clark. We did a sweet four-way and opened about 1,800 feet, way off the airport. I tried to make a run for the airport with a 7-TU, but was backing up pretty fast.

I was headed for the railroad tracks and power lines, so I turned and headed for a patch of green. I barely cleared some huge trees and hooked it into a small piece of grass besides this big fancy building.

I stood up the 7-TU and immediately cut away one side to keep from being dragged. Four armed soldiers and several guys in suits came running toward me.

I was scared shitless. What the hell was going on?

Apparently I had nearly landed on Eisenhower's tomb and the Secret Service didn't think it was funny. I explained the situation as best as I could, and they escorted me out of the Memorial.

Two questions still haunt me about that jump. Why would a dead president still need Secret Service protection? And if he doesn't, is perhaps DDE still alive?

Dempsey Morgan

The Day My Reserve Streamered …Three Times

I enjoy the warm knowledge that many of my skydiving buddies have also experienced phases in their lifetime of jumping when adolescent mentalities trumped basic safety concerns.

In 1978 in Dalton, Ga., I was jumping an SST with an RW round and a 26-ft. Navy conical. On one opening, I was more than a little surprised to see a gnarly stabilizer entanglement that had me in a pretty brisk turn for a round. The canopy had proven to be uber-reliable, but apparently I had finally managed to bungle the pack job sufficiently to blow its record.

Years before, I had stayed with a partial that nearly ended up killing me, so this time I elected to get on with it and cut away.

Sitting below my beloved but unmodified 26-ft. Navy conical, that I had jumped too many times, I proceeded to engage my four-line release system that was modified. To save money for more jumps, I had rigged a four-line release with loops of 550-cord securing the back four lines to each connector link that I would cut with a hook knife, thus sparing the suspension lines from being cut. It worked great, but I couldn't get anyone to pack it. Had to work around that.

I cut the loops with a razor and took off. The four-line release on a conical delivered significant drive—faster than most rounds, but it turned like a dog.

As I was flying along, happily looking for a place to land off the DZ, from out of nowhere my reserve folded up and went into full streamer! My heart stopped completely! What a way to go. I didn't have a lot of options. As I plummeted downward, staring wide-eyed at the streamer and pondering the reality that this would be my last living sight, the canopy popped open!

I was shook! I stared madly at the open canopy, looking for cause, and before my eyes the front of the skirt pushed into the middle and the canopy collapsed again into full streamer. This was so unfair; it shouldn't be happening. I was given a reprieve and had it yanked away. But again, after we had built up a good, brisk vertical speed, the canopy popped back open.

Fortunately I hadn't opened low because the canopy streamered yet again. I was nearly going insane over the injustice of the thing.

Now I was completely desperate, down to a few hundred feet and fully expecting another streamer before I got to the ground. I steered toward a grove of trees, hoping the canopy would snag the branches before impact, and low and behold, I would make it there before the next collapse.

But what looked like trees was actually a vine covering over ten-foot cedar trees that I blew through and stood up unexpectedly.

The rest of the story: I had also saved money by using a small folding razor from my advertising work instead of an expensive hook knife, and the sharp tip of the blade had nicked a *fifth* line, severing it to give me the hot five-line-cut that I can verify goes a little faster than it should.

If I hadn't slowed the drive by making turns to hit the trees, the canopy would have collapsed again at a couple hundred feet. At least I didn't repeat that stupidity.

Buzz Ansley

I Was Hoping They Could Shoot Straight

We did a series of demos at the Wildlife Preserve in Largo, Md., in 1975.

On one skydive the spot was off, and it was unclear where we'd land. By the time I was at 300 feet, the lions were standing on their hind legs, paws against the tall chain-link fence that separated their compound from the park visitors and our intended landing area.

The big cats were staring up at me under canopy, licking their chops, I think. I was under a PC, not a ram-air. The park staff had their tranquilizer rifles ready, preparing to put the lions down. On final, I was hoping they could shoot straight.

I cleared the fence and the lion compound by maybe 30 feet, and changed my underwear shortly after.

Andrew Gillinson

He Musta Thought He Was a Goner

SCENE: Wallace's Drop Zone and Spa in Crosby, Texas. Summertime, 1960s. Temperature at 100 degrees Fahrenheit, and with humidity at 99 percent, Houston is hot.

SUNDAY: Six to nine of us are attending sky cathedral. A new guy drives up in a rental car. He has *all* the correct gear and parachuting equipment. Even a packing mat! Tidy! Squared away ... wearing spiffy duds. He packs his parachute like a brain surgeon. The sincere sort, he says: "Hi! Checked with the FAA and found your NOTAM!"

He manifests himself for a jump; explains his air hero status, the Yankees he knows, the miles he's driven, the skies he's conquered. Our good luck. Puffs 'n preens gracefully ... a humble sort in his own dreams.

Like a Samaritan, New Guy offers that any two of our paltry skydivers who might accomplish a two-way formation in *freefall* ... well, then, *he* would close third to grant our DZ a three-man star-shaped formation! Now he had our rapt attention. Skippy is *delighted!* Cheery! Gleeful! A wonderful opportunity! Carlos signs on as the third man.

TAKEOFF: The Cessna C-195 lifts skyward, heading for 7,200 feet to a rousing chorus: "Hoot! Hoot!"

EPIC SKYDIVE: Carlos and Skippy hook up just out the door. After a polite pause with ceremony, New Guy flies in, entering third. Magic! A three-man Star! Yawn. Overwhelmed with devilment, Skippy and Carlos transition the three-man star into a three-man line. Welder's gloves enable tight grips. Carlos Gene has New Guy's arms. Skippy owns New Guy's legs. Hot Damn! ... *Giggle-giggle* ...

MULTIPLE SKY WONDERS: Voila, the three-man line! Rare! The poetry and joy of three-man RW flight is profound. It merits "OMG" moments! New Guy is particularly excited. Writhing, kicking and screaming, he's having the time of his life! He shakes like a belly-dancer.

CATCH & RELEASE: At 800 to 900 feet, satiated, Carlos and Skippy let go of New Guy above Houston dirt. Texas scenery flashes upward; bushes freight-train up as trees run away! With the ground rushing up at his face like D-Day at night, New Guy deploys his parachute with alacrity.

CAUSE: Flagrant safety violation! By coincidence sun-struck, two bored Texans experience a temporary judgment lapse, but do deploy their canopies at a low altitude.

CORRECTIVE ACTION: Such safety defilement curdles the Parachute Club's Safety Officer (CSO) into fetid cheese. However, our CSO did not freak out. Mostly because we never had one.

NEW GUY: Canopy open, he lands and scurries to collect his kit. Awestruck to the hilt, he stuffs everything in the rental car and splits.

LATER: Stalwart true believers weigh heat and humidity versus hope, and manifest a five-man star formation shot from church at 7,200 feet. Cool. As in one-and-a-half miles up, it's cool over a Houston DZ in summer's fierce heat.

Pat Works

Adrenaline Kicked In

It was my 44th jump on April 12, 1973. No shit, there I was … in a violent spin under my brand new Cloud. The spin was so bad that my body was prone to the ground. All I could see was a crumpled yellow and black ball of garbage screaming at me!

The first time I tried to grab my Capewells, I failed. The centrifugal force was so strong I underestimated the strength it would take just to reach them! I thought to myself that I'd better get it together and fast!

The second attempt was a success. My adrenaline kicked in and I could have ripped a car in two!

Off I went across the sky as my reserve came out. A loud, sudden "Pow!" and I was sitting under my round reserve.

I looked down, ready to hit the ground, but to my surprise I still had plenty of altitude left. What seemed like minutes had been just a fraction of a second! *Woo Hoo… defied death again!*

I never felt more alive after I landed.

Lloyd Tosser III

The Hawaiian Sinking Adventure

Guy Banal, a good friend who was a well-known French chef working in Oahu and who jumped at Perris Valley and Elsinore every time he was in California, invited me to Hawaii for a local boogie in 1989. It was held at Dillingham Airfield on the north part of the island; the field was separated from the ocean by a road.

On the morning of the third day, we had a 21-way planned. We let the locals spot as the winds were blowing inland in the morning and out in the afternoon, and a spotting mistake could put you on the slopes of a volcano or in the water.

Knowing that we would be jumping over the water, I was wearing an inflatable life vest (the type you get from a commercial airplane when they fly over the ocean.) I had had it for several years, probably since my water jump when I qualified for my D license in 1980.

I had been jumping for a while with lead weights in a harness that I wore underneath my jumpsuit and could access from the front. I could choose how much weight to put in it, in units of two pounds. That morning, looking at who was going to make base, I decided to use all of them, or 12 pounds.

We got out at 12,500 feet, and I was one of the last to exit. Diving out I noticed we were a little distance from the island, but I figured the up-stairs wind would bring us in. We made a 19-way formation, and when I looked down, the island was farther away. *Uh oh.* We broke the formation at about four grand, and everyone tracked toward the coast.

People started opening at about three grand, and I did, too. A normal canopy appeared. But I noticed that the glide ratio on my Hobbit was not very good compared to the other jumpers. I was sinking faster than they were and not making as much headway.

Within a few minutes, I knew I was going to make a water landing. So I prepared. I had a lifejacket so I wasn't worried. I am not a great swimmer, but that's why I was wearing flotation gear. I thought of dumping the weights. That would have been the prudent thing to do, but I planned on making more skydives with those guys and without the weights, I'd have a hard time staying with them. So I kept them on.

I loosened my leg straps and noted the size of the waves. I knew that altitude could be estimated from just looking at the distances between the waves. But, by looking at the coast ahead *(shit, was it that far away?)* and the angle it made with my point of view, I was pretty sure I could cut away a few feet off the water. Which is what I did when I got close.

I splashed down, and the water was salty. I came up to the surface and made sure that I didn't get entangled with the main, but I kept my rig on. I looked for the black inflation tube leading to the life jacket and began to blow into it.

Suddenly I realized I'm blowing and blowing and the jacket is not inflating. *Uh oh*. I'm holding the tube and it's not attached to anything. Shitty glue? Too old? Man, no one told me those things aged! By now, looking to the shore, I saw that most of the jumpers had made it to the drop zone, though one or two landed on the beach.

Okay; change of plan. Time to get out of my gear, but I hadn't loosened the leg straps enough and I couldn't seem to free myself. The webbing was now totally soaked, and it wouldn't slide through the hardware. Rather than fighting to get the rig off, I decided to just start swimming toward the shoreline.

I swam and swam and swam; I got tired. I stopped and noticed that while I wasn't floating easily; my head was just barely under the water. So after every breath or so, I kicked up, breathed in, sank down and bobbed up. I kept repeating this routine, but about 15 minutes later I was quite exhausted and barely closer to the beach. I noticed I was still carrying the black inflation tube, so I tried using it as a snorkel to breathe while I rested.

Still, I was totally exhausted. I mean, I was dead flat out of energy. Not being a strong swimmer, I wasn't surprised. As I rested with my head below the water while breathing with the tube, I started to think that I wasn't going to make it. Strangely enough, I was quite fine with that. I was dead tired and my thinking process was working just fine, but my energy level was past any reserves I had left.

Just then a wave pushed me a bit higher, and I saw a surfer approaching. It was a woman—she was about 100 yards away and moving toward me. Okay, I decided I still had enough energy to stay afloat for another two or three minutes.

When she paddled up to me, I was so happy to place my hands on her board. I then recognized her as a local jumper who I remembered from Perris in the early 1980s. She was this cute blonde, with long hair, thin, and very nice looking. I forget how she had landed on Oahu, but I was certainly glad to see her at that moment.

After 10 minutes or so of her towing me in, I finally could stand in the shallow water. The drop zone staff was there with a van and people who were going to swim to get the missing folks. I was lying with my back on a coconut tree, and folks were removing my rig and opening my jumpsuit.

Oh, shit. The weights! I had decided not to dump them when I was at a grand because I had the lifejacket, but once I hit the water I never thought about them again. No wonder I was so tired and had a hard time keeping my head above water. I had 12 pounds of lead dragging me down.

But I was still carrying the black inflation tube.

The ambulance arrived, and I was given oxygen. At the hospital they checked my oxygen and it was at a low level. The doctors there told me I was the first person they had seen who was still alive with such a low oxygen level. I was seen all day long by different doctors who wanted to gawk at the near-zero oxygen guy. They kept me there all day.

Driving back to the DZ, I was told that the winds that morning were blowing the reverse direction and the locals had not noticed such a rare change. Because it was a 7 a.m. jump, the beach was totally deserted except for the woman who rescued me. I forget exactly why she was on the beach, but most likely she was a surfer looking for a good wave.

The next day, I was still too tired to jump. The DZ staff had cleaned and repacked my gear, hoping I was going to jump with them until the boogie ended, but I was not feeling well enough.

Now, Guy was wearing a new lifejacket. He said he had never worn one until that day, but if that shit could happen to me, he figured it could also happen to him.

Philip de Louraille

I Was Already Dead

I was in a two-way with my good friend. In freefall, okay? She had only 100 jumps and I had over 2,000. The skydive was a follow-the-leader jump, where I would do a freefall maneuver and then she would follow with the same maneuver.

Right out of the plane, we faced off and I did a back loop. When I came out of the back loop, she had disappeared. Then I felt her crashing down on my back. She had been unable to stop her back loop and I had drifted underneath her. Her knee hit my spine, causing a spinal contusion. I was at 10,000 feet and unable to move my arms or legs. I was completely conscious. Until 3,000 feet, I tried to move my arms to pull my reserve handle.

I could not move.

I said to myself: *"I am glad I have a Cypres."* My next thought was: *"Did I turn it on this morning?"*

I could not remember if I had turned it on or not. Realizing that I was at the mercy of my AAD or that I was already dead, a strange calm came over me. Just then a flat spin began to develop. Soon I was seeing ground, sky, ground, sky. At 700 feet a white flash went past me, and I was suddenly under my reserve. There were line twists from the steering toggles to the canopy. I tried kicking out the twists, but my legs did not work. I tried reaching for the steering toggles, but my arms did not work. The reserve was a 210 sq. ft. Tempo and it flew straight, even with line twists.

A telephone line flashed by and my canopy snagged on the line. This stopped my forward motion for a couple of seconds. Then the parachute slipped off the line, dropping me into a planter between a spiked fence and an asphalt road. I landed flat on my back on my still-packed main. The fall must have pushed my spine back into shape because I could wiggle my toes and move my fingers.

I stood up. A man in a truck came speeding up to where I was and said, "I never saw anyone open that low in my life."

"Neither have I," I answered.

"What can I do for you?" asked the man.

I said that I could use a ride back to the drop zone, and climbed into the back of his truck. Back at the DZ, my freefall companion was sure that I had gone in and that she was responsible. We ran into each other's arms in happiness and relief.

No shit. There I was. You can't make up this kind of story.

Rick Thues

Heart-Shaped Formation

My favorite NSTIWTIWGD story is a night dive in 1977, right after the Nationals.

We were all tuned up from team jumping and thought it was a good time to go for the world record night circle jump, which stood at 19 or 21 at the time. We had 22 jumpers on board. We wasted some prime beer drinking time because the moon didn't actually rise until 10 or 11 that night … something we didn't account for initially.

In addition to the normal altimeter and helmet lights, we had reflective tape on our jumpsuit wings. Mike Jenkins had this big strobe light and he wanted to make sure we had a good picture. I took the extra precaution of breaking open a glow stick and outlining my reserve ripcord.

The circle built to about 19 and funneled. There was a lot of vertical separation but very little horizontal. Nothing worse than 22 skydivers wandering around the sky at night looking for a place to pull.

I tracked away and looked over my shoulder, only to see three or four jumpers above me silhouetted by the moon. I decided to keep tracking and take it down a bit before pulling to be sure that nobody stopped in to say hello rather abruptly.

Around two grand or so I dumped, but my Piglet opened into a streamer. This Piglet had streamered before, including a few times when I was able to pull apart the lines and it would open. I also had a few cutaways on the same canopy, and one where my thumbs were in the rings and the opening shock *(where did that come from?)* jerked my thumbs down and I was back in freefall. A guy on the ground said it opened just after I left it and I said, "Yeah, that's right." But I digress.

I was trying to separate the lines when I remembered that I had already dumped low and decided to cut away. After cutting away, I had the comforting sight of my reserve ripcord glowing in the dark. The opening was hard but welcome.

I was at 500 feet; a couple more seconds and … ouch!

About half of us (not me) wanted to go up and try it again. By this time it was one or two in the morning. I said my reserve wasn't packed so I couldn't go. Don Hansen piped up and said he had a backup rig I could use.

Now there was something I wanted to do: go back up after the first attempt funneled, I almost died, in the middle of the night, borrow somebody else's gear, and try again. Having said all that, I did agree to go but the majority of the group wanted to turn in and that was what we did. I was relieved.

Every time I show the photo to whuffos, they ask if we were trying to build a heart-shaped formation. I tell them "No, that is the start of the funnel" and tell them the story. That was my last night jump.

John Jennings

This Is Painful

Okay, NSTIWTIGD … but not until after the jump was over.

I had just bailed out in a pretty dark cloud over The Ranch. We were at 14-grand, and the clouds were pretty thick and patchy. On jump run the Otter was all over the sky, as in *"fasten your seat belts,"* so I knew we were in the middle of some weather.

On a GPS spot, I didn't see ground anywhere. At any other DZ, the pilot would likely abort the load. But this was The Ranch, where the rules are just rough guidelines. There used to be a sign here saying that the only rule was that there were no rules.

I was doing a two-way with a low-time guy who made his first jump at age 60. We got out, I went after him, he disappeared, and we were in a full-bore hail storm. *Woo-hoo; this is painful!* I had been in them before, for maybe 10 seconds. This one went on for 30 seconds.

Amazingly, we got out of the soup and I found the guy, hooked up with him, and we did a few points. I opened in blue sky around 3,000 feet. My face felt like it had been slapped silly.

When I got on the ground, my face was full of welts. It was the same with everyone else on the load that didn't have a full-face helmet. The guy I jumped with said my jumpsuit belly was completely iced up when I came in to hook up.

Doug Garr

One Step At a Time

NSTIW, at Elsinore, with Hallam. I guess this was around my jump number 20. I had become expert at lying flat and stable for base, so today we were going to do something different. We were going to exit at 12,500 feet and practice me pinning him. He was going to hold on to my harness on exit so as not to waste time getting together. Then he was going to back away and let me pin him, then back away further and further after each pin until it was time to pull.

Walt Cleary was our pilot in the old Howard 418. A couple of other jumpers got out on our way to altitude. Hallam and I were the last to exit. We got to 12,5 and I spotted. I gave the cut to Walt, he throttled back, and I got out. Once I was in position, Hallam grabbed my harness and yelled, "Three, two, one, go."

Hallam jumped and I froze. I was now hanging with Hallam on my harness. I was holding up myself, my rig, Hallam, and his rig. I looked in the door and Walt was white and yelling at me to let go. Hallam was yanking on me and yelling, "Let go."

I looked down and saw the step right under me. If I let go with Hallam holding on to me, I'd surely hit the wheel with my face or head. I yelled to Hallam to let go of me as I tried to kick him off. He wasn't letting go, and the look on Walt's face was scaring me.

By now we were almost to the lake; I had climbed out over the drop zone. Suddenly, I felt a tremendous jerk; I wasn't sure what was happening. For an instant I was dazed and confused. Hallam had jerked me so hard he broke my grip on the plane.

I went straight down and hit the wheel and step head first. I heard a deafening crunch. Hallam still had hold of my harness.

We fell clear of the plane; he turned me around and his eyes got huge. He was pointing to my head, and then I saw blood on my goggles. I was feeling okay, so I motioned him to let go so I could pin him. He let go and backed off. I pinned him and nodded that I was okay. We continued the jump as planned and we both made it back to the DZ.

Once on the ground, we figured out where the blood was coming from. I had hit the plane with my brow bone. I had a one-inch cut just below my left eyebrow. That was lucky because it could have been my eye.

When we got back to the DZ, Walt came running over almost in tears apologizing; he didn't know what to do. He also said when I finally let go and hit the plane, it rocked to one side. Then he turned to Hallam and cussed him out for not letting go of me. It was kind of weird seeing mild-mannered Walt so pissed.

I went to the ER at Elsinore, got a few stitches, and was ready to go up again.

Sandy Harper-Calliham

Run For Your Life

Here is a NSTIWTIWGD story that took place entirely on the ground.

Around 1977 I worked for United Airlines, and went to Hawaii to make some jumps at Dillingham Field. One of the jumper's girlfriend flew the sail plane rides for the tourists. He talked about six of us into going out to the end of the runway and mooning her and the tourist passenger as they landed the sail plane.

The sail plane was about six feet off the ground, moons were full, and the tow plane was about six feet off the ground on final. Everyone was laughing and looking behind as we soon realized that the sail plane tow line had snapped and the remaining line was dragging along the ground behind the plane.

That line was headed right for all of us.

You have not lived until you see a bunch of mooners, with their shorts around their ankles, run for their lives in every direction. All escaped the line as it passed us by, snapping down the runway behind the plane.

I always wondered if that tourist got full altitude for that ride.

Craig Myers

Perfectly Good Airplanes

You don't even have to leave the ground to have a NSTIWTIWGD story. I have three of them:

I'd just gone to work for Bob and Judy Celaya in Cal City. It was a typical hot and windy afternoon; I was teaching the AFF FJC and Hank Asciutto was teaching a static line FJC. He was finished first but had to leave, so I took his students up.

We got into the C-182 and taxied out. I won't mention the pilot's name as he's a damn good pilot and a friend of mine. One of the students was a really big guy so I had him with his back to the panel, and I was kneeling between his legs facing forward. We lined up on the runway; the pilot added power and we started rolling.

We got up to about 50 mph and the nose wheel was just getting light when the pilot slumped over the controls. I reached up and shook him but he was out cold. I grabbed the yoke and the throttle and actually thought about continuing the takeoff since we were going so fast. But my measly 100 hours of flying time and the fact that I couldn't get to the rudder pedals made that a no-go.

I pulled out the throttle and kept the wings level with the yoke as best I could. But we were quickly veering off the runway. Then I felt one main gear leg fall off the edge of the pavement and off we went into the weeds. I'd only been at Cal City a few days and wondered, *"Is there a fence on this side?"*

I tried pushing the student out of the way to get my hands on the rudder toe brakes but I don't think he realized what was happening and he was fighting me. I think he thought I'd gone berserk and was trying to push him out the open door.

We were bouncing around like crazy and still going at a good clip when I managed to get one hand on the pilot's side right rudder pedal and the other hand on the left one behind the student. But that was ass backwards so we did some serious swerving before I figured it out. I was trying to apply the brakes evenly so we didn't ground loop into a fiery wing-over. We finally came to a stop in a cloud of dust and dirt and everyone was all right. The pilot came around and it was just a case of dehydration and not keeping the water pumping on a very hot day.

* * *

A somewhat similar thing occurred when I was working in 1980 down at Borderland in San Diego. The DZO was the very first DZO I'd met I didn't really like. He was a mercenary—just in it for the money.

On the Saturday sunset load the jump step cracked and fell off his C-182, but first thing Sunday morning it was fixed. I didn't think anything of it and took up four loads of static-line students. On the last load we were running out of daylight so I didn't take the time to pack and rode the plane down wearing an emergency rig.

We landed and turned off the runway. If you jumped down there about that time, you know how rough that dirt strip was. I was sitting in the door with my legs dangling outside and considering my first cold beer of the day when suddenly the right-side gear leg snapped right under me and down we went.

It pinned my legs under the fuselage. Lucky for me the dirt was soft. It didn't hurt me and everyone came running to lift the plane off me. It turned out that the DZO, being a cheap bastard, had decided to fix the jump step himself. His not being a certified aircraft mechanic could have crippled me.

The sprung gear legs on most Cessna planes are heat-treated parts, but he didn't know that. So when he welded the step back on himself, he didn't realize he was weakening the gear leg itself. That last landing and roll-out was all it could take. I was a qualified mechanic and would have gladly fixed it right for him, but he knew he'd have to pay me.

* * *

This last story is a bit hairier. In the same vein, it didn't actually include any jumping. I was working for Don Balch in Hemet, where we had a really cool kid named Chip flying for us. It was winter and getting chilly when one morning I came to work and Chip said, "Hey Nick, I built a roll-up door for the Cessna last night. Will you go up with me and test it out?"

Sure. The plan was to simulate some jump runs rolling the door up and down few times. The door was essentially several steel rods and heavy plastic sheathing; the rods were wider than the door with Velcro on the bottom to hold it closed. When I looked at it I said, "Wow, Chip, this is kind of overbuilt."

But up we went. Larry from Bonehead Helmets was there, too. He was just a ground video dubber back then. To this day, and I know I knew better, I'll never know why we didn't take rigs with us, but we didn't. After all, we weren't jumping—we were just going flying.

We climbed up to 3,000 feet and Chip started a simulated jump run while Larry and I were just sitting in the back on the floor chatting. I handed my cup of coffee to Larry and got up on my knees to roll up the door. I rolled it up; I rolled it down. We did some lazy eights with it up and down and it worked fine. So I secured it down and we started descending to the airport.

Then all hell broke loose.

As we picked up speed on descent, the door suddenly blew out. It turned sideways like a thing possessed and smashed into the window behind the door, showering Larry with plexiglas. Then it turned vertically, and the steel rods started punching holes in the bottom of the wing. After it ruptured the bottom of the fuel bladders, we began getting showered with gasoline. Chip was freaking out: "Oh shit, Don is going to kill me, Don is going to kill me!"

I yelled, "Shut up and keep flying the plane." I handed Larry my coffee and told him, "Grab my belt and hang on." And I climbed out on the strut to try pulling the door back inside.

Remember, I wasn't wearing a rig. I was absolutely drenched in av-gas, and the door was beating the crap out of me, but I managed to get hold of it and pull it back in. Then it took both Larry and me to hold it down on the floor until we finally landed.

When we rolled to a stop, happy that the plane didn't blow up, Larry tapped me on the shoulder. When I turned around he smiled and handed me my coffee cup. He hadn't spilled a drop.

Nick DiGiovanni

So, Of Course, I Looked For a Gun

This event occurred some 40 years ago in Mexico. It wasn't my fault; I drank too much Mescal, became eight feet tall, and decided I was made of iron.

Shortly after I exited this quaint whorehouse by jumping out the window, the villagers of Guadalajara gathered to chase me; it was apparently some sort of local custom. So, of course, I looked for a gun. Afterwards, I jibbered, jabbered, did some reds, and went to bed.

Next morning I had a hangover. I got up and staggered to the bathroom to piss. Being sewn to an unnoticed mattress made me pause in the door until the stitches broke loose. Shortly thereafter, we did a demo skydive into a soccer stadium at 5,000 feet with a panicked pilot who sweated mucho. Fedo spotted, took a snort, and shouted: "Cut! Give me five-left and a glass of water!"

Since missing the stadium meant landing in a deep canyon, I compensated and pulled a bit low. I got open at about 75 feet.

Later Fedo, while inhaling energy-producing powders and running backwards, took the orphan kids on a brisk run around the soccer field. Tattooed and attired in his blue jean denim hat, with purple bandana, gold chain, a purple mesh-net tank top, and crotch-split shorts (with his balls hanging out) bounced up and down, shouting, "!Viva boogie! … !Viva Mexico! … !Viva Boogie!!"

Later that night Fedo won about $500 at a mob scene cockfight. He had a bad flu so, naturally, to maintain the party mode he took acid to ward off the flu's effects. It worked. He didn't sleep for three days. Luck and I covered his six a.m. departure for the airport when it was time to head home. Fedo wisely ingested several reds and two or three chloral hydrates to induce restful slumber.

When the departure was delayed, he ended up in a coma on the terminal floor—pale, white, and drooling. Only a coordinated team effort, including my soulful on-the-knees begging, got his body released for the flight home. Entering the States, U.S. Customs cheerfully took apart all our luggage and parachute gear, and strip-searched Dan and David. They found about a half pound of white powder in the pockets of our jumpsuit legs.

"What is this?" they asked. We replied honestly: "That is just tortilla flour that we put in our pockets and jumpsuits for the demo jump so we could be seen better as we skydived into the soccer stadium for the poor orphan children … blah blah blah."

We were held until another guy in a dark suit and tie came in with a very interesting expanding suitcase. He measured and mixed up the powder in various vials; carefully swirled them around, and then closed up his suitcase. He stood up and said, "Tortilla flour", and departed.

Back home, it took a while to rest up. Fedo awoke four days later, refreshed.

Pat Works

Pretty Stupid on My Part

Casa Grande ("Casa Gulch"), Arizona was the site of a NSTIWTIWGD moment or two back in the mid-1970s.

After a day of building big ones with Jerry Bird and company, one of the pilots wanted to impress the crowd with a buzz job. He snuck up on us by coming directly out of the setting sun.

I was standing between two buildings, about 50 feet west of a wooden utility pole. This guy came across the DZ in a twin-engine Cessna at max speed, directly over me. He got lower and lower until I hit the deck out of fear of a cranial prop strike.

As the plane roared past me, I heard a loud cracking sound and turned to see that his left wing had come off as it shattered the pole. The shadows in front of him had obviously masked the pole until the last second when he started to pull up, albeit too late. But doing so caused the plane to slowly spiral upward for its final arc across the road before crashing.

That was NSTIWTIWGD moment one.

NSTIWTIWGD moment two was when I ran through the fine mist of av-gas to get to the crash site.

Halfway there I realized that if something in the debris set off a spark, I would be instantly broiled alive. Pretty stupid on my part. Thankfully, there was no fire. Unfortunately it was a moot point for the poor pilot, may he rest in peace.

Phil Mayfield

Don't Leave the Cameraman Hanging

I think I had about 50 jumps or less. I was just hanging around Elsinore one day when Don Henderson was talking to a guy named Pete Dickerman from Germany. It was Pete's last day before going home and he wanted Don to film his opening.

I overheard the conversation and asked Pete if he ever had a kiss-pass. Pete said no, so I offered to jump with him. We planned to do a quick two-way and kiss-pass, and then Don would film his opening. I was to break off at 3,500 feet so Don would know the altitude and could concentrate on the opening shot.

Pete wanted to pin me, since he hadn't done much RW. I believe we went to 7,500 feet. We exited the plane and I laid base for Pete. It took him forever to get near me. He was on my level, but just couldn't close without going low. He kept looking up at me, and that made him backslide. So I decided to go after him. I was intent on catching this guy. Hey, there was a kiss-pass at stake!

I never even looked at my altimeter. I was just concentrating on pinning this guy and getting a kiss-pass. Finally I nailed him, gave him a quick kiss and looked at my altimeter so I could wave off to let Don know it's time.

Holy shit! My altimeter read way into the red. I'm talking about 700 feet or less. As I waved off and came in to deploy, we were over the DeJong Dairy behind the hangar. This is no lie: I was so low I could see the tits on a cow. I had so many things going through my head at this point … but I looked up, got line stretch and opened.

I heard two more pops, looked down and saw two canopies open below me. The lowest was Don, who barely got line-stretch and landed. Pete was above him. I was at the top and a few seconds later, I landed in a cow field.

I got out of my gear as fast as I could and ran over to Don, who hadn't moved. He just sat there. The first thing he said to me was, "What the fuck were you trying to do, Calliham, kill me?"

Pete walked over and wasn't even shook up. He was talking about how cool the kiss-pass was and couldn't wait to see the photos. As Don and I gathered our gear, he said, "You know we're going to be grounded."

I said I didn't care because I was still shaking, happy to be alive, and not interested in jumping right then.

When we got back to the DZ, there was Gary Douris. If looks could kill, we were both already dead. He told us that someone yelled "They're going in" —and from his viewpoint, all three of us went below the hanger before opening. Everyone thought it was going to be a triple bounce.

Some said by the time they ran around to see us, only I was under canopy and about to land.

Gary told me that I wasn't getting in a jump plane for a month. I told him he didn't have to ground me because I was going to ground myself. I needed a month to think about what had happened.

The following weekend Don came to see Bill and me at home. He brought the photos of the jump. They turned out really good, too, and you could see how low we were. He said I'd show you the opening shots, but I ran out of film right after the kiss-pass.

The moral of this story is two-fold: altitude awareness always, and don't leave the cameraman hanging.

Sandy Harper-Calliham

Can't Beat Luck

Floyd probably never thought he was going to die on an historic skydive.

He participated in the first baton pass made by Canadians in 1959. (The first baton pass had been made by Americans in Canada the previous year.)

Floyd's jump, however, was not without incident as, after passing the baton successfully to Daryl Henry, he free fell into Daryl's parachute on opening, knocking himself unconscious.

Luckily, both ripcords dislodged during the collision and he descended unconscious under his main and reserve.

Ilona Helwig

Nobody Was Dead and Nothing Else Mattered

We were doing night jumps at Perris; my group was on the last load of the evening. It was late, probably past 11 p.m. when we put out a few solo first-time night jumpers at 7,500 feet before climbing to altitude.

On the way up and under the full moon, I noticed it was beginning to get really cloudy below us. By the time we turned on jump run, we were totally socked in. Of course, there was no GPS in those days, so we did a couple of go-arounds looking for a hole and a landmark, but there was nothing below us but solid clouds.

I made my way up to the cockpit to speak to the pilot, Ron Webb, and told him I couldn't see anything below us. I believe we talked about making some kind of jump run using the March AFB VOR, but both of us quickly realized how dangerous that could be. One reason was at the time we didn't know how thick the cloud cover was. Also, there wasn't exactly a load of sky gods in the back. It was just your average bunch of weekend fun jumpers, with me being the senior jumper.

Then I realized we had another problem. I was looking at the instrument panel in the Otter and it was kind of bare. It had the basics for VFR flight, airspeed, horizontal horizon, compass, but nothing in the way of IFR stuff. And I'm sure Ron was already thinking about it, but it struck me right then to ask, "How much fuel do we have?"

Well, it turned out since we were to be the last load of the night, we had the fuel to make the jump and enough to divert the plane to a local alternate airport if needed, but not much more than that. Ron suggested we try one more pass at a jump run, but if that didn't pan out we'd have to go find another airport to land.

I walked toward the door, explaining the situation to everyone as I went. I was smiling, you know—keeping it light, but I was worried big time.

We made another go-around, but again there was nothing but solid clouds. I closed the door as Ron banked the Otter right and we headed off toward the Hemet airport. But Hemet was socked in, too. And by this time Ron was on the radio; he found out everything alternate within our fuel range was closed to all traffic.

It was all zero-zero.

I had a decision to make. Sooner than later we'd be forced to descend into the clouds, which I was sure Ron would do before we ran out of fuel. So it would be a controlled descent into what? Should we stay in or get out? In the area we were flying it's fairly open, but there are also mountains, water, houses, freeways, power lines, and who knows what else. If I knew for sure we were in the valley over Perris, I might take a chance on a south or north jump run, but since we flew towards Hemet I had absolutely no idea where we were.

Everyone was looking at me.

I decided we'd jump. I figured either all of us, or at least most of us, would surely survive. If we stayed and the Otter plowed into a mountain or a building, none of us would. It was all about probabilities, just pure math. I was about to explain it to everyone when Ron waved me forward. "I'm going to declare an emergency and land at March Air Force Base," he told me. "They can guide us down."

I knew what he meant. There was a tower there that was manned all night, and they could talk us down using a PAR approach. March was also closed to all traffic, but once you declare an emergency they can't really say no. Basically the controller would be using radar and telling Ron on the radio to "increase your descent, slow your descent, come right five degrees, come left five degrees…" until we hit the runway. And all that in a solid overcast that went right to ground level. A lot was going to depend on Ron, but I trusted him.

I went back, told everyone we were going to land at March, and made them put on their frap hats. Not many wore real helmets in those days. I also, and probably for the first time ever, thought *"Damn, I wish there were seat belts in this thing."* We were in the clouds now and descending. And I could feel Ron maneuvering the Otter to stay within the controller's instructions. When we got to a thousand feet, I opened the door halfway so if anything happened we wouldn't be trapped inside.

When my altimeter got down to a couple hundred feet I couldn't help but brace myself, and noticed everyone else did, too. We touched down firmly but not all that hard, and as we rolled out I could barely make out the runway lights. Everyone onboard was cheering like crazy. But it wasn't exactly over yet.

We came to a stop and I fully opened the door to see armed men, lots of them, approaching us out of the mist. At that time March wasn't just any Air Force base. It was a Strategic Air Command—or SAC—base and they launched B-52s loaded with nuclear weapons day and night. Several men approached the open door with M-16s pointed directly at me. I must have been quite the sight with my Chem Lites glowing away.

"Who are you and what are you doing?" one of the men barked at me.

"We're skydiving," I said.

"At night?" he said back to me incredulously.

They ordered us to stay in the plane and we did. Then some of the jumpers on board began needing the bathroom. I was actually surprised that it took so long to come up, as I'd been ready to piss my pants for the last half hour. I learned later they were keeping us on the plane until they woke up some officer to take charge of the situation. I politely them told we had some women on board (and quite a few men) that were about to pee their pants. But these guys were deadly serious and having none of it.

Finally they allowed us off the plane, and along with Ron they marched us off to a small building where we were allowed to use the facilities. And then they had Ron on the carpet.

There was a colonel there, and he was super pissed off. In effect, we had committed a serious breach of security and the colonel's ass was in a sling. Ron was taking the brunt of it; they took him away into a side room and I heard the colonel screaming that Ron would have to remove the wings from the Otter and truck it the hell outta there!

Ron returned, looking a bit glum. We were basically held captive all night. When morning came, the weather had cleared and there was a bus waiting outside to take us back to Perris. We left Ron and the Otter behind. I wasn't sure what happened next, but I heard the colonel eventually went home and some enlisted guys gave Ron enough fuel in a bunch of five-gallon jerry cans to fly back to Perris.

Back at the DZ, where I thought we'd all have a big laugh about it, they were pissed off at us. Several of the jumpers on the load had brought children with them to the DZ that day, and the staff was stuck babysitting all night.Ben had gotten a phone call from the Air Force, so he wasn't smiling. But I was happy as a clam. Nobody was dead. And nothing else mattered.

Nick DiGiovanni

Opening Shock Was Devastating

During August 1965 a number of gliding parachute designs were being constructed and tested, but none had been jumped from an aircraft. That changed, however, on August 6 when I jumped the Barish Sailwing at the Lakewood Sport Parachuting Center in New Jersey.

I had secretly tested the Sailwing with 18 jumps, and was ready to demonstrate it at the U.S. Nationals at Orange, Mass. The Sailwing was determined to be flying and opening well enough to parachute into the meet on the evening of August 23.

Lyle Cameron wrote in *Sky Diver* magazine: "The wing banked and *flew* to the Friendship Bowl," and admitted that Jacques Istel, the president of Parachutes Incorporated, had "pulled a completely secret chute out of the bag."

The military showed great interest in the Sailwing, and invited David Barish and me to demonstrate it to a group of military and government officials the following year on April 24. The two Sailwing parachutes at Lakewood were tested the day before and both had malfunctioned. I called David and told him he should reconsider going to Dayton, Ohio, on the following day, but he was adamant about being there and told me to get them out of the woods, choose the best one, and be in Ohio with it the following morning.

I told him that I did not want to jump it under these circumstances, and he said we would pack it up and talk about it in the morning at Wright Airfield.

It turned out to be a good morning for me because the weather prevented the demonstration from taking place. The ceiling was 2,500 feet and the ground winds were steady at 25 mph with higher gusts. David said that I should get in the airplane, establish an opening point, and he would cancel the jump because of the unsafe conditions. We took off in a Cessna 205 from the Darbyville, Ohio, Skydiving Club. The pilot was unaware of my intention to not jump the rig that David and I had so carefully packed an hour earlier.

From the airplane we watched the buses arrive and unload the passengers of military and government officials who filed into the grandstand. There was a white canvas cross just a few yards in front of the seated spectators. The control tower notified the pilot to proceed on jump run; he turned and shouted to me that our prayers had been answered. (Not *my* prayers.)

There was a break in the clouds and we would be able to get the 4,500 feet we needed to make the jump. I accepted my fate and got out on the step, knowing that the ground winds were no problem for the Sailwing but that landing with a reserve canopy in the event of a malfunction was not an option, especially when considering that the approach to the grandstand was a solid formation of cement buildings.

I exited and did a five-second delay, all according to the script. Because the Sailwing opened so quickly it was imperative that you pulled subterminal, but it was just as important to exhibit to the people watching the demonstration that this was a freefall parachute jump. The Sailwing was absolutely not to be opened at speeds of 125 mph or more.

With all this in mind, the ripcord was pulled at the appropriate time, but nothing came out of the backpack. It felt like a total. By placing my hand on the bottom of the pack, I located the two flaps, put my fingers under them, and then pulled the flaps apart until I got the pilot chute on its way. By now I was 10 seconds into freefall and my body position was head down because my hands were still behind me during the opening sequence. The canopy was pulled out with such velocity, and my body position was so bad, that the opening shock was devastating.

Unbelievably, the Sailwing opened without any damage and was facing directly at the grandstand. It was flying brilliantly. But, because the opening was approximately 1,500 feet lower than the planned opening at 4,000 feet, it seemed that even the Sailwing would have a problem covering the distance to the target from that altitude.

With the saddle of the harness pulled up behind my knees and my hands and elbows pulled tightly into my body, resistance to the air was minimized. The chute's amazing forward speed of 25 mph, combined with the wind speed of 25 mph, created a ground speed of 50 mph—unheard of under parachute at that time. I flew past the control tower at this speed and recall that this was breathtaking and something I had never experienced.

Still moving forward at this speed, I passed over the spectators in the grandstand, which created an incredible experience for all who were below me. At approximately 100 feet above them the Sailwing made its first turn during the entire flight! It banked into a smooth left turn and faced into the wind, neutralizing the ground speed to zero and allowing me to land gently, standing up a mere 20 feet from the center of the target.

Considering that the flight of the Sailwing began at approximately 2,500 feet, almost two miles away, this proved to be nothing short of a miracle. All of the people on the ground had no idea of the many problems I experienced during that remarkable demonstration of accuracy, and believed that all had gone according to plan. A huge contract went to David Barish Associates.

Lee Guilfoyle

Public Education Can Be a Good Thing

It was the summer of 1968, and I was doing a night demo. The first time I did a night demo, we used 30-second hand-held flares. Yep, you guessed it; I looked straight at the flare right when I struck it on exit, and couldn't see diddly-squat for almost the entire half minute it burned.

Luckily, our exit was from above 8,000 feet and thanks to a public education, I knew enough to count and opened at 1,500 feet.

For years I didn't tell anyone how dumb I was on that demo.

The next night we went out lower, and one of the guys on the load dropped his hand-held flare on opening. It flamed out just as it bounced.

The people on the ground that were watching thought someone had just bought it. They came running over to the guy that dropped it and said that one of the jumpers had just gone in.

His response was, "Sorry about that, folks. Can you give me a ride back to the airport so I can repack?"

Dennis Henley

When We Hit a Rock

There was a Twin Otter load in 1983 at the Perris Turkey Boogie that was certainly a NSTIWTIWGD ride; I thought we were going to crash.

I loaded up close to the door. Someone had garbled the seatbelts so I ended up with only half a belt—one end with no mate.

Of course, that's when the right engine decided to explode at about 60 feet, sending fragments everywhere. I asked my seat mates on both sides if they'd share their seatbelt. Both were big-eyed and said, "No!"

So I sat on the floor and grabbed onto legs. Our great pilot, who had thousands of hours flying fighters in the military, did a very scary go-around with a soft but very high-speed landing.

We'd slowed to a near stop, when we hit a rock.

Pat Works

So-o-o-o Low

It seems like my jumping days were kind of sedate compared to some of the wild and crazy antics in the sky I've heard from my fellow skydivers. I did have a few close calls, such as when I had to raise my knees to my chin to avoid some electrical wires, barely clearing them; also, I had a night jump that scared the shit out of me.

That jump was on August 19, 1978, at Perris out of a DC-3. I jumped solo and was prepped and briefed by Bob Celaya before the jump. I had all the glow sticks and chem lights, everything I would need to successfully complete this night dive. I was hyped up and ready for the first nocturnal leap of my career.

After I exited I was blown away by the bright stars, close enough to touch. However, almost all of my lighting gear blew away, too, so I was mostly in the pitch black, not able to read my altimeter. That kind of unnerved me, but I figured I had been falling for about 20 seconds, so at about 2,500 feet, I checked for other jumpers, saw that I was alone, and pulled my main. It opened without a hitch.

Everything was perfect. I was again enjoying the view, looking around at other jumpers in the distance, and began to focus on the landing area. All of a sudden I heard a *Shhhhoo* sound not ten feet from me; someone was still in freefall. I finally heard a canopy opening not far from me. I couldn't believe someone was so close to me, had almost hit my canopy, and opened so-o-o-o low. It had to be below 500 feet; she had a very short canopy ride, practically nonexistent.

Yes, we all landed with no problems. I chatted with the gal who opened so low; she said she didn't know where she was or at what altitude—she just did a Hail Mary opening.

Well, I loved the experience, but losing the lighting gear freaked me out, as did the close call with the other jumper. So there were a few seconds there when I felt NSTIWTIWGD.

Mary Stage

Then Things Took a Turn for the Worse

Back in about 1987 I was the chief instructor at Lake Elsinore (Debbie Blackmon was the DZO) when we received our first tandem rig from Ted Strong. At the time none of us had ever laid eyes on a tandem rig, but Debbie already had some tandem customers scheduled for the following day.

I was busy teaching that day's AFF first jump course, and Debbie thought sending two experienced jumpers up on the tandem would be a prudent idea as a pre-check of the rig. (I'm not sure, but I don't think there was an actual tandem certification course at the time.)

To us, it was just another parachute system.

I taught my FJC a few times while the guinea pigs looked over the rig. Then they took the rig to altitude. The next time I saw them, they were in freefall at about 1,500 feet with nothing out, not even the drogue. Suddenly, the main appeared; it sustained major damage and they landed in a heap, both shaken up but alive.

It turned out the "tandem master" either couldn't get the drogue out or, more likely, just forgot to deploy it. So when he pulled the main, of course nothing happened.

The bottom guy had been frantically clawing over his head, trying to find the reserve ripcord when the top guy finally clicked as to what was happening. He then managed to get the drogue out but since the main container was already open, the main deployment was brutal.

Blackmon took the now blown-up tandem main back to her loft and worked through the night to repair it. The following morning she asked me to take the tandem rig up and test her repair work. After the previous day's fiasco, I took the rig into the empty classroom, along with the manual, and studied how tandem rigs really worked. I decided to jump it solo as I thought there was no reason to risk two lives.

Bob Metz was flying the Beech when I hopped aboard with Ernie and some others who were on their way to a local demo. On the way to altitude I went over the procedures, touching handles and thinking things through, with an emphasis on getting the drogue out, as that was yesterday's big problem.However, as it turned out I was too focused on that part. Bob rolled the Beech onto jump run at 12,500 feet and I got in the door, spotted, and got out thinking, *Deploy the drogue, deploy the drogue!* Which I did straightaway.

Suddenly, bang! The rig tightened around my body and I thought, *Man, that drogue has a hell of an opening shock.* Then I noticed I was completely de-arched and the horizon was in the wrong place—what the hell was going on here? I looked over my shoulder and there was the Beech right behind me. I'd thrown the drogue way too early and the bridle was wrapped around the tail of the plane.

I was in tow!

I noticed Ernie looking out the door at me, his eyes wide as saucers. I got a hold of myself and remember thinking, *Okay Nicky, nothing really bad is happening right now, so don't make a second mistake that may kill you or everyone else in the plane.* I looked down at all the handles on that rig and was kind of horrified to realize none of them did what I needed to do.

So I went for my hook knife, thinking I might be able to cut the drogue bridle free. But my hook knife was on my personal rig sitting on the ground. It was the only time I'd jumped without one and the first time I really needed it.

Then I noticed Ernie and rest of the load bailing out but now, at least, I had a plan. I was going to pull the cutaway handle on the main and then pull the drogue release. It was all I could do. I knew I'd be leaving Bob with a mess hanging off his tail, but it seemed like the only answer. Then things took a turn for the worse.

I noticed the horizon was sinking in relation to my feet as the Beech began nosing over into a dive. I looked over my shoulder and saw that the landing gear was coming down. And that told me two things: that Bob Metz was still at the controls and we were in deep shit! On many occasions I'd heard Bob tell newer pilots, "If you don't know what's happening when you're flying the Beech, put the gear down!"

I glanced at my altimeter; we'd lost 3,000 feet really quickly. And we were picking up speed. I had to get the hell out of there. I took a bit more time figuring things out (remember, I'd never even seen a tandem rig before the previous day) and then reached for the main cutaway handle. I was just peeling the Velcro when suddenly, and inexplicitly, I came free and was in freefall.

I was passing through 8,000 feet. I looked up and saw I had a trailing main bridle but no drogue. I thought about just dumping the reserve, but was concerned about an entanglement with the bridle. And I thought since I hadn't pulled the cutaway handle, I still had a shot at the main if I could get the main bag off my back. I pulled the main drogue handle but it only moved a little bit and jammed.

I pulled as hard as I could, but it wouldn't budge. (Unbeknown to me, while in tow the cable on the main container three-ring had been sucked through the grommet and locked it up.) I dropped the main handle and grabbed the secondary one (the passenger one) but that one was jammed, too. I looked at my altimeter; I was going through 5,500 feet. I decided if I got to four grand, I'd just pull the reserve, no matter what.

I went back to work on the main release handles. But this time I grabbed both of them and pulled with my last ounce of strength. And they came free. The main bag floated up and hit me in the back of the head. I reached up and pushed it away as hard as I could, and then watched in slow motion—more like suspended animation really—as first the lines came off one side of the bag and then the other.

Hurry the hell up! I was thinking. Finally, the bag came off and the main canopy opened. I actually took my first breath then, at least consciously anyway. My altimeter read 3,000 feet.

I landed and watched the Beech land too, thankfully. All the guys on the demo were accounted for. There was a big dent in the forward section of the Beech's horizontal stabilizer.

The pilot weighed in: "I was just sitting there," Bob began, "when all of a sudden the yoke was pulled outta my hand and slammed full forward. No matter how hard I pulled, I couldn't get it back." [The wrapped bridle had pinned the elevator in the full up position.] "With full up trim and full power, we weren't level but we were holding our own.

"Then the demo load exited the plane and the loss of weight in the back did us in. That's when we really started nosing over, and that's when I put the gear down in order to try slowing us down. But that wasn't really working and I was just considering getting out myself when you came free of the tail."

Metz and I drank a goodly amount of beer that evening and Debbie, being Debbie, took the cost of a new tandem drogue, bridle, and bag out of my next paycheck. Naturally it put me off tandems for a while; it wasn't until 1994 when I finally got a rating and started doing tandems for real.

The lessons are, of course, tandem isn't just another jump, and when someone comes up with something new you know nothing about, run like hell as far away from the DZ as you can.

Nick DiGiovanni

He Called Out the Marines

In 2011 at the SOS World Record gathering for seniors, I had a malfunction; poetic justice for going low on a sixty-something-way. While the Elsinore rigger was packing my reserve, I had to rent gear. The pro shop asked me for my driver's license; I was in a rush to get on the next load.

Cut to Sunday night. I was at LAX on the security line, two hours early for my flight back to the east coast. When I got to the first TSO officer with my boarding pass, she asked for my photo ID. *Uh-oh.* I left it at the gear shop!

I fumbled around my wallet. Very politely, she asked me to step aside. Another security guard came up because I was now a problem. He asked what I had in my carry-on. Um, a sport parachute. Oh shit. He called out the Marines.

In a one-hour huddle with various TSOs; they inspected the gear, begging for a photo of me. I signed all the FBI and CIA forms and waivers, whatever, allowing them to invade my past.

Finally, I found an expired contractor's card with a photo, but it said 'Douglas' and not 'Doug.' It didn't match the boarding card. More huddling. Finally, they took a vote … should we let this guy on the plane with his parachute?

Moral of the story: Don't forget your photo ID when traveling.

Doug Garr

So Much for War Surplus Equipment

In September 1962, I was making my third jump after going through the static-line course at Elsinore. My first two static line jumps were Zs; I went over backwards and the canopy deployed between my legs.

There were two other jumpers going to 7,500 feet—Linda Padgett and her husband, Wayne. I was making a 10-second delay with a stop-watch on my reserve. I was a little nervous about letting go of the strut on the C-172 with one hand to punch the stopwatch, so I asked Wayne if he would reach over and start it. He looked at me kind of funny, as in *"Are you serious?"*

But he did it and off I went. After about five seconds of freefall I started Z-ing out, so I went ahead and dumped. Well, I was already starting to go over when the chute began deploying. I watched the whole thing play out and wondered why it was taking so long for the sleeve to slip off.

Then the whole thing began whipping around like a jump rope, with the pilot chute holding one end and me the other. In a couple more seconds I thought, *Oh shit, this thing ain't ever gonna open*. I was on my back looking up at the pilot chute when I pulled the handle on my reserve. The flaps peeled back but the canopy just sat there on my belly.

My first reaction was to punch the canopy to one side to get it into the air. All this time I had the feeling that the ground was about to come up and smite me; finally the reserve started deploying. It took a while to inflate. For a second or two I thought it was going to wrap around the main, but it finally opened.

I found out later that Linda was kind of shook up because they watched everything and thought I was going to bounce. I also found out that the main pilot chute had two panels blown out and thus couldn't pull the sleeve off the canopy. So much for war surplus equipment.

John Granados

The Day I Almost Bought It

The year was 1974. We were doing an exhibition jump at the Van Nuys Airport. On the load were Charlie Sweeney, Jay Sweeney and me, jumping out of a small helicopter from 4,500 feet. My rig was a Pioneer Hog Back, with a PC main and a 26-foot conical reserve.

Plan: make a three-man. We got the two-man, and three was slow; suddenly I looked at my altimeter which said 1,200 feet. We broke, I pulled my main, looked back, and had a pilot chute hesitation. I reached across and got the reserve. I knew I was a goner, as the runway numbers got real big. I thought: *"Well, it's been a nice life."*

Suddenly I felt my knees bend sharply as I hit the grass area next to the runway. My reserve had beaten the main out. And in doing so, it had burned its side all the way up to the apex. I never got a secondary, as rounds do, because it had a built-in modification.

Big tears came free-flowing out of both eyes as I was swarmed by the ground crew. The tower actually got a picture of the main and reserve in a streamer at 250 feet. So my reserve opened just above the ground. By some miracle of God, I had a relatively soft landing.

The lesson learned, of course, is "When in doubt, get it out." If I hadn't pulled the reserve, I wouldn't be around to tell a NS story. But just imagine having to say that a pilot chute hesitation got me.

Chuck and Jay were open below a grand and we were very embarrassed in front of hundreds of people watching the air show. We gave them a good one. It should have been filmed for Gypsy Moths.

Stan Troeller

Long Live Pink Floyd

I never, not once, jumped stoned … on purpose.

But one day at Perris, not too long after I began jumping again after a one-year layoff (due to a broken back,) we had just enough jumpers to make a sunset Twin Beech load. Just as I was about to climb aboard the airplane one of my gurus, a very famous skydiver who will remain nameless, handed me something and said, "Here, eat this."

I never even looked at it, let alone asked what it was. I just threw it into the back of my mouth and swallowed it.

If I remember correctly, it generally took around a half hour to 45 minutes to get to twelve-five back then, with eight jumpers aboard. It being a sunset jump, the pilot decided to keep climbing until the sun went down. It generally took me somewhere between 20 minutes to an hour to start feeling the effects of LSD, and this was no exception. When we finally got on jump run, my Guru looked at me and asked if I was as messed up as he was, and then someone shouted "Go!"

I didn't fully realize how loaded I was until I got out the door and everything took on this psychedelic look. I must have peaked because of the long ride, little blood circulation, and adrenalin because it was the most beautiful and incredible thing I had ever seen. As I went into a dive, I just put myself on autopilot and went with the flow until I got down near the formation. I must have gained a little bit of awareness because I didn't even try to close. I just flew around it, awestruck.

I remember thinking that if everyone in the world would go skydiving and see what I saw, there would never be any more war. About the time I began thinking these deep thoughts, the formation broke and everyone went tracking off.

Being somewhat paranoid, I pulled high; that canopy ride seemed to take hours before I did a nice soft standup landing.

Everyone was walking back to the packing tables since there was nobody left on the DZ to drive out and pick us up. My Guru walked over and asked me if I was getting off; all I could do was look at him and nod. I always felt a little paranoid when tripping so I did something I had never done before. I threw my unpacked canopy and gear onto the back seat of my car and drove home to Quail Valley.

My guru showed up in a few minutes and we had a great laugh at what had taken place, but the more I thought about it, the more it scared me. Later that night we had a small party with a few very special invited guests, and during the party my guru and I talked at length about it. He told me that he had jumped high several times and that they were his most favorite jumps of all, but I decided that it wasn't my cup of tea. I never did that again.

I used to worry about the LSD doing some sort of genetic damage, or having some sort of flashback. That's what everyone warned us about back then, but since I have two very healthy and normal children and haven't had a flashback in all the years since I ate my last LSD, I guess I made it okay.

But I owe a debt of thanks to Owsley, or whoever it was that invented the stuff. It gave me a perspective on the world that I couldn't have gotten any other way.

And yes, I still like psychedelic rock. *Long Live Pink Floyd.*

Criss Morgan

I Couldn't Swim

NSTIWTIWGD – December 17, 1969, Cedar Hill, Texas.

I needed a water jump to qualify for my D license. Bobby Crump, our pilot and inspiration for "Crump's Jump Bunch", warned me that I had to land my cheapo smack in the middle of the pond or he would not sign off on it.

Did I mention it was December 17th?

But it was a warm day, and I had just turned 18, all full of myself. I did a damned good spot, even if I do say so, and hit the bull's eye.

As soon as my feet hit the water, I found out that 65-degree air did not translate to 65-degree water. As my head slipped beneath the surface, my throat closed involuntarily and I couldn't breathe due to the cold.

My feet became entangled with the lines. With the weight of an inverted canopy, I couldn't swim. I spotted my buddy, Richie "The Mexican" Grimaldo, laughing and snapping pictures on the shoreline as I managed a meager *"HELP!"*

It was the first time in my life that I knew I was about to die. Miraculously, though, I struggled my way to shallower water, as I was about to go under for the third and final time. If I'd had more energy I would've kicked Richie's ass.

But I got D-2629 shortly thereafter.

Ken Mayfield

I Fell Out Of an Airplane and Lived To Tell About It

I had my first reserve ride, if you can call it that, on a malfunctioned 24-foot unmodified military surplus reserve. This is the true tale of how I got the nickname "Turtle" when I was in a body cast for nine months. I made my next jump exactly a year to the day after this fateful skydive.

Cliff had flown his Twin Beech to Perris for a weekend of jumping; he got there in the middle of the day on a Friday. There were just enough skydivers to make up a load, so we hurriedly geared up and climbed aboard. What we didn't know was that nobody was left in the manifest shack to communicate with the airplane. This was to make a major difference in my jump that day and probably contributed to the circumstances that saved my life.

The climb-out took a long time—we probably got 13,5—but what we didn't know was that during the climb-out, the Santa Ana winds came up with a vengeance. We figured later that the wind speed was between 45 and 50 mph.

The jump went fine: a nice eight-way star that we broke off high. But when my PC opened, it had a radical turn to the right. I looked up and saw there was a stabilizer lock. That happened once in a while, so I was a little slow in trying to clear it. It had always come out with just one yank on the lines, but this time no amount of pulling would clear it. I had been taught that when in doubt, whip it out, so I cut it away.

But I pulled my reserve at precisely the worst possible time, face-down instead of falling back-to-Earth. The pilot chute went straight down, then did a U-turn and came right back up into the reserve that had deployed on either side of my body. I reached both arms under the right hand side of the canopy and rolled to the left so the canopy could go where it was supposed to go—that is, up. Everything was tangled when the canopy finally grabbed a little air. When it opened as much as it was going to, I thought I was going to die.

Incredibly, the pilot chute had somehow gone between the risers of my belly wart and tied itself off at the skirt. So it had the entire right hand group of lines tangled off, and the apex of the canopy was pulled all the way down to the skirt on the right hand side. I had basically half of a reserve, and not a very big one at that.

Man, it was one of the scariest things I had ever seen in my life. I fought it all the way to the dirt, to no avail. All I can remember was my desperate cry, in what sounded to me like a growl of masculine rage (but was probably more like a mousy little squeak.) I kept saying, over and over again, "Not Die, Not Die."

I didn't say, "Don't Die," just "Not Die." Don't ask me why.

Because of the extremely high winds I was blown way off the drop zone; I landed in the proverbial freshly plowed field. I have pictures somewhere of me laying there on the ground, hurting and waiting for the ambulance to arrive.

If I had landed on the hard-baked earth of the airport, it would probably have been curtains. There were three clearly visible points of impact—craters, if you will. The wind was blowing me sideways so fast that the impact was spread out and dissipated a little at a time with each bounce. I also might have done the best PLF of my life. The combination of the sideways speed, the soft ground, and maybe a good PLF all together saved me.

With all due respect to those who have gone before me, I have seen people die that had a lot more canopy open than I did that day. It just wasn't my time, I guess.

Here's a strange coda to the story: One of the guys on the load was named Ski. He was a U.S. Air Force Para-Rescue team member, and the first one to reach me. When I came to, the weirdest thing I had ever seen was this figure running toward me. My arm blocked my sight of his head so all I could see was this headless black jumpsuit running to where I was. I thought it was The Reaper, and it scared the hell out of me.

Then I remembered it was Ski, and that if anyone in the world could keep me alive it was him. There was also this Marine Corps Gunny; I am ashamed to admit that I can't remember his name. He was sort of short and stout, and he used his fist as a pillow for my head the entire time I lay there waiting for the ambulance. I thought it was some sort of miracle.

But even though I was hurt badly, I lived to tell about it. I wound up with a severely broken back, all the ribs on my right side broken, and a fractured leg. I was grateful it wasn't worse.

Every night, while in the hospital in Riverside, a group of jumpers would come to visit me. I was there about a month. One night Al Frisby smuggled a bottle of whiskey into the room, and another night my first jump instructor, a man named Jim Craig, a lawyer from San Diego, brought me the finest looking cake I have ever seen. It was shaped like a girl's torso—one with a great figure, and she was wearing a very tiny bikini. One side of the bikini top was pulled off and it exposed ... well, you know what. In the next two days, before I cut the first slice off the cake, every nurse, doctor and student nurse in the hospital came by my room to look at it. And they also came to see the guy who, according to the Riverside newspaper: "Fell out of an airplane and lived to tell about it."

If anyone who reads this knows Jim Craig, please get in touch with him and let him know I still have great memories of him, and how good it was to have known him. He was a really good guy.

You can also be sure that I never did another cutaway without being in the correct body position. Plus, I never jumped a chest-mounted reserve again.

Criss Morgan

Wrapped Me Up Like a Burrito

Earlier in the day, Alan Richter and I saw Mark Sechler and Tim Long hooking up their canopies in flight—a Paradactyl pinned by a Strato-Star. We decided we could do it, too.

On the next load, Alan pinned me under my Piglet II with his Strato-Cloud. Well, that was at about 1,500 feet after the usual 2,000-foot opening. It only took a few seconds, but that Cloud slammed into the back of me and wrapped me up like a burrito. Who would have thought a Cloud would fly so much faster than a Piglet? At about a grand Alan looked up and said, in typical Alan fashion, "Hey Rick, I think I'm going to cut away."

I said, "Me, too."

We let loose with our fancy new three-ring Wonderhogs, *Woo-Hoo*, and we both cleared the tangled canopies. It felt sooooo good. I was really happy to be free of that Cloud; I arched and smiled and took in the clean air. Then I realized I was going through 500 feet. I saw people on the ground pointing at me. I swear I could see their fingers.

I pulled the blast handle on my Wonderhog and a beautiful 24-foot flat circular opened about 200 feet later. Of course Alan, the chicken, pulled right away and made me look low. I *hate* that. My reserve swung twice and I landed (on the down swing, of course.)

Alan and I hit the ground running—we knew who was going to be looking for us—but we were no match for the old man. Bill Stage came for us like Clint Eastwood busting through the saloon doors chasing down a couple of dirt bags. He found us hiding between the packing tables, reserves in our arms, with that *"you lookin' for me?"* look on our faces.

Well, after that safety meeting, Alan and I had our own; it was well deserved.

Rick Ford

Good Strong Teeth

This is a NSTIWTIWGD story whose main character is a hook knife.

I was 19 and jump-mastering a student load out of a C-182. I had a student in tow. He was slowing spinning at the end of his static line and was not showing any signs of consciousness.

In those days, the emergency procedure for a conscious and responsive student was to cut the static line and the student would pull the handle on the front-mounted reserve. If the student was unresponsive, the jump-master was to use the carabiner we all carried on the main lift web to attach himself to the static line and then slide down it to the student. You would then cut the static line and deploy the incapacitated student's reserve.

This script was actually in *The Jump Masters Handbook*. Whoever wrote it had obviously never tried to do it because when I did, there were a number of issues I'm sure he didn't anticipate.

The student was not only a heavy weight on the end of a rope, there was considerable air speed drag involved, too, pulling that static line extremely tight across the floor and around the jamb, down the fuselage. You have to clip on well outside the plane, or you're not going anywhere. I figured this out and finally clipped on after considerably bloodying my knuckles.

Already I was thinking that this wasn't fun. I rode down the static line, smashing face first into the still-spinning student. Our bodies were 180 degrees out of alignment, both of us facing away from the relative wind, both slowly pinwheeling, winding up the static line like a twisted rubber band. I couldn't reach his reserve handle in this position. Meanwhile, I looked down and noticed we were descending, no doubt from all the drag we were causing.

I figured the student was a goner because I was running out of options. I used all the strength I had left to push myself away from him, trying to get a clear swipe at the yellow dope rope without cutting his harness with the blade.

Finally, I felt a *Ka-snap* and he was gone. I guess the combination of my pushing off in terror and the ever-tightening winding static line freed whatever was holding the container closed. As I watched the sleeve come off his back and lines unstow, I heard a *Boink* and felt a sharp snap through my body.

The student was gone, his T-10 catching air, so I thought he'd probably land okay. But I was still swinging like Tarzan behind the 182. There was a bunch of white nylon slapping my boots and an MA-1 pilot chute in my crotch. Since I had a blue hot-dog pilot chute on my main, I figured somehow I'd popped and shredded my reserve.

I figured at this point I had two options. I could cut the static line and go for the main, hoping it cleared the remnants of my 23-foot Tri-Conical reserve, which obviously I couldn't release. I was too low to hack at it with the hook knife, which I suddenly realized was still firmly clutched in my teeth (which is where I put it while back on the plane's step when this adventure started.)

The second alternative was to crash land with the plane, hoping that getting dragged at high speed down the grass strip wouldn't kill me. We were in a right-hand descending turn right over the pea gravel, low enough that I could see the guys all looking up and pointing.

Plan B was not very attractive, so I cut the static line, dropped my knife and pulled the main ripcord with both hands. I closed my eyes as I flipped over and cart-wheeled away from the plane. An instant later I was in the saddle, my Rainbow 252 overhead in perfect position for an accuracy run at the disc. I was only 500 or 600 feet off the deck. And there I was, right on final.

Well, I made the pit but missed the disc (I had nothing left in my arms to sink or flare the canopy.) After I stopped shaking, we started putting together what had transpired.

I was getting chastised for not pulling my reserve since I was so low. I yelled back that I no longer had a reserve, pointing out how it was damaged during the ordeal. The club's president then walked up to me and pulled the reserve handle. I stood there dumbfounded as the reserve fell off my back onto the ground.

My wrestling match with the student somehow blew his container open, and as he fell away the weakest point remaining was the sleeve retainer line which tore apart, allowing the T-10 to open clean, free-bag style. This left the sleeve and pilot chute still attached to the static line. The MA-1 bridle caught up against the carabiner clip on my harness, the white cotton sleeve trailing and flapping away.

When I cut the line, the drag from the mess cleared everything away from me and I was simply in freefall (rather low) with an undamaged and completely workable rig.

The student was fine and, in fact, most likely didn't know anything out of the ordinary had even happened until he started picking up on the debrief. The pilot thought I had become disabled and was headed to the open plowed field across the runway from the peas. He has going to cut the static line up on his end at around 500 feet. Being a real considerate type, he didn't want the guys to have to walk too far to find my body.

The following week someone found one of those orange rubber-handled hook knives in the grass next to the target area. I told him it was mine, and I wanted it back. He said. "There's no name on it, how do you know it's yours?"

"Look at the fuckin' teeth marks in the handle," I said.

Jim Twardowski

Life Was Perfect

Let me start by saying that Jim Bohr scared the crap out of me. I always thought that at any moment he would kick my ass just for the fun of it.

According to my log book, this jump was on August 12, 1974—my 232nd jump. It was a three-man scrambles in Rainbow, Wis. They drew names and as luck would have it, I was on Jim's team along with some wide-eyed new guy. We decided to just throw him out as base.

Suddenly we were socked in; the scrambles were called off in what looked like an endless weather hold. The next thing I knew, I'm doing bongs with Jim in his van. We were so loaded. As I lay in the van listening to Pink Floyd, suddenly I heard the planes winding up. The scrambles were on. I had to help Jim find his rig!

I had visions of death going around in my mind. I had never jumped stoned before. As we got close to jump altitude, we were dodging little thunderheads. Jim was kneeling next to the pilot and spotting, directing the pilot toward a large dark-grey thunderhead. The pilot, who was wearing a baseball cap, was shaking his head 'no.'

Jim grabbed the back of his neck and squeezed. I guess he was afraid of Jim, too, because the next thing I knew we were being buffeted around inside this rather angry cloud.

Just as I had finally come to terms with my demise, we came out on the other side. There was the DZ. Out we went and it was an awesome jump. It was a great jump, really fast! And as soon as I hit the air, all the fear was gone and life was perfect.

Lloyd Tosser III

You-pull-lower-than-me-and-you're-dead Smith

It was in the days of rounds and belly reserves. I had been jumping with my mentor, Bill Smith, up at Fulton, N.Y.

For those who don't know him, "Smitty," as he was known, had a reputation for opening low. It was not undeserved, as safety officers grounded him all the time. He'd simply move to another DZ until his period in isolation expired. In fact, the legendary Dan Poynter gave him a nickname: "You-pull-lower- than-me-and-you're-dead Smith."

Smitty and I were doing a two-way from 7,500 feet. He frequently jumped without an altimeter, keying on much saner skydivers who opened at the proper altitude. I probably had 150 jumps at the time, flying a PC Mark I that was tricked out for accuracy.

We did a hook-up, broke off, and were facing each other in freefall at about three grand. He took the ripcord handle out of its pocket, waiting for me to dump. But he had that look of a gunslinger backing off on Main Street. He was actually backsliding and grinning.

He was challenging me to a low-pull contest. Though I was young and pretty brash, I wasn't stupid. I sort of obliged, but I wasn't in it to win it, if you know what I mean.

I checked my altimeter, took the ripcord handle out of its pocket, and when we reached 2,000 feet I pulled. I waited and waited for the main to come off my back. Nothing. It was a NSTIWTIWGD moment. A few seconds later, Smitty, likely seeing my pilot chute hesitating, dumped his main. I watched him go up. I was now thinking—that's a pretty long pilot-chute hesitation.

But I didn't know whether I'd had a total. As a last-ditch effort, I went into one of those panicky sitting positions, shaking my pack left and right. I was well under 1,500 or so, and the main finally shook loose. When I got the welcome opening shock, my pulse was at max rate and I was well below Smitty's canopy—an all-red PC. Very befitting of this skydiver, the Red Baron. I can't ever remember landing before him until that skydive.

I had opened lower than Bill Smith and lived to talk about it. Smitty loved to tell that story again and again, but he never revealed the salient fact that I had blinked well before he did.

Doug Garr

Scotty Carbone Saved My Life

We were at Z-Hills, somewhere back in the fog of time, and everything about this jump was strange. There were low clouds, so we had a strange exit altitude—like 6,800 feet or something like that.

It was a five-way, which was also kind of strange. But the most dangerous part was that there were four guys and one woman on the load. So, of course, we four guys were all going to impress the low-time newbie young beauty with our manly skydiving skills.

I remember we pretty much instantly built a four-man and then started to fly it over to the young lady who was earnestly doing her best to get to us. Just before docking she reached and floated up and away, so again we slid our four-way toward her. In reality, all we wanted to do was catch her eye, steal her heart, and in some imaginary fantasy have her bestow the honor of a "happy ending" upon some lucky one of us.

But the stark reality was that it almost turned out to be the end of all of us. Suddenly, right in front of me, in a flash of colors I saw Scotty disappear as he was dragged up and out of the four-way by a deploying main. Now we all know and love Scotty for his many exploits. But I also knew that Scotty was red hot as a skydiver, and if he pulled right out of the formation, then there must be a really good reason.

So I looked down, and I swear—there was a house the size of a shoe box racing up at us. I instantly dumped, didn't turn, didn't track, didn't do anything else but dump. The canopy opened and as I reached up for the toggles I hit the driveway and actually rolled out onto the front lawn.

In pain I was lying there looking up into a sky with just one parachute overhead, believing that everyone except me and Scotty were gone. I got up and felt my sprained ankle. I started hobbling around to the back of the house where I heard voices. Amazingly, everyone else had landed right there behind the house in the adjoining backyards.

The only problem was that the lovely young lady was standing frozen in place, with her parachute draped up and over the backyard power line. We yelled, "Don't move!" and someone (and it wasn't me) cut away her main. She just walked away.

I don't remember ever seeing her again or much of what happened after that. I do know that back at Z-Hills, they said they saw one parachute open and then watched a four-way disappear behind the tree line.

That's the day Scotty Carbone saved my life, and that's why, no matter what, I will love him forever.

Mike Sergio

OMG! Did You See How *Low* We Were?

In 1975 at a Conference Meet at Elsinore Jan Works, Daryl Defreitas, and Tommy Owens asked me if I wanted to do four-way competition with them. *Did I?? OMG! I'm a 100-jump wonder, wondering what I'm doing! Of course, I would!!*

Our first jump was a four-way/break/back-loop/two-way cats. Sounded easy enough. We dirt-dived it, felt good about it, and went up in the Howard, ready to do our stuff. (We all wore conventional gear, by the way.)

Our exit altitude was 7,500 feet. On the way up, Janner had some problem with her contact lenses, but she seemed to get it all worked out. The exit was fine; we built the four-way pretty quick and broke grips. Did the back loop. Tommy and Daryl got the two-way around three-grand. It took a few seconds for Jan and I to get on their legs. While I was flying in to Daryl's legs, he sat up some as I slid in, and that put me right on his back.

I was laying *on* my right arm, bouncing around in his burble, unable to get my own air. We fell like proverbial rocks. I was unable to get my arm out so I could pull, and we plummeted … yes, plummeted … through a grand.

I was wiggling like a snake, trying to get off Daryl's back. I finally got enough room to push away from him. I reached in to pull, looking into his eyes as I did. He fell away from me as I opened and lost sight of him. When I looked down I saw him far below me, at least it seemed that way. Then I looked at my altimeter; I was at 800 feet.

OMG! I'm low … Jesus, I'm low! I landed and went over to Daryl, continuing to repeat myself: "We were *low*, did you see how *low* we were!! OMG…"

He was standing there daisy-chaining his canopy, a lil' smile on his face. I was still freaking out and going on and on and on about how *low* we were. Well, we were at the bottom of Rome Hill *(we were low!)* As we walked back, I kept mumbling about how damn low we were. We caught up with Janner and Tommy. I'm still going on and on and on about how low we were. *(Shut up already, Deli!!)*

We sauntered … yep, sauntered … back to the DZ. We started to pack and then heard over the loud speaker: "Would the four-way that opened over by Rome Hill please come to the manifest."

I looked around to Daryl and Tommy: "Are they talking about us?"

"No," Tommy said, "couldn't be us" … so we just kept packing. Then this guy (Gary Douris) walked over to us. His face was sooooooooooo red. He looked at us, shaking his head back and forth. He pointed at Tommy and yelled, "Who was on the top?"

Janner and Tommy raised their hands. He looked at Daryl and me and said "You two are *grounded!*"

Then he looked at Janner and Tommy: "You two are *warned!*" (They were open over a grand.)

I started to sputter: "Can I tell you what happened?" He yelled at me *"NO!!!"* and walked away.

My first meet and my first jump with Sky Gods, and I got grounded! What a hell of a way to start my Skydiving career!

Chris Deli-Schilpp

A Night in the Desert

It was a NSTIWTIWGD night jump: I jumped into the Nationals in Marana, Ariz., out of Spanky's Beech at around midnight in 1969 with a group from Los Angeles. We used the pool as our point of reference because that was the only big bright thing outlined with lights that we were sure of.

We had no idea of the wind conditions on the ground (turns out it was blowing from 100 feet down.) I thought I could see the direction in which the planes were tied down, so we used that as the direction for jump run. In reality, Spanky knew all along in which direction to point us. He was just putting up with all of our corrections until he got tired of us calling them out, and then he said, "Time to get out."

When I got to down to about 60 or 70 feet, I could see that all of the plants were running in the wrong direction, and faster than I expected. I did a last-chance 180-turn back into the wind to try and slow down a little on landing. At touchdown my main wrapped around a bush, so I didn't need to cut it away.

At zero dark thirty the desert is very cold, so I slept wrapped in my main and had some of it propped up over that bush so the rising sun would not beat down on me. I had some candy and a beer in my leg pocket, so I was all set for breakfast when I got up. We ended up landing all over the county and it took until sometime in the light of morning to get everyone rounded up.

Dennis Henley

That Was One Jump Too Many

When I bought my SST Racer, Audrey Jackman showed me how to pack the main. She also told me that Racers were a bit peculiar. They were very sensitive to body position at opening time, and I had to be careful that the pilot chute didn't end up on my back, caught in the burble.

The other difference with the Racer was that once you pulled the "rabbit" pod (which was attached to a rather flimsy inverted pilot chute,) you had positively opened the pack. The bag housing the main was now free to go. The prevailing wisdom was that if you have pulled the rabbit pod and the main did not deploy, you must cutaway regardless because the main could still deploy and the last thing you needed was a main-reserve entanglement.

Also, that inverted pilot chute was attached to a pod which was located at the bottom of the rig, right on the butt, and which attached via a Velcro patch to the rig. It was not always easy to reach all the way down there, at least for shorter-armed folks.

Lastly, with one's arm fully extended to reach that far, there was not much strength available to complete the pull. If your rig had been closed tight, pulling on that rabbit pod to pull the pin to open the rig to free the pilot chute could result in more than your share of hard pulls.

So when it was time to open, I was always a bit nervous while thinking: "Time to save my life, let's see if it works out!"

I had three jumps on the Racer and I was not happy with the openings. I was deploying with my right arm and I am not that tall, so I would see it hesitate, or flutter, and then I would bank slightly by looking and maybe making the situation a bit worse. But the main would open after a few seconds. Of course, back then, bigger jumpsuits were in vogue so the size of one's burble was bigger and more chaotic.

On my 103rd jump (my fourth jump with that new two-day-old rig) I pulled the rabbit pod and threw the pilot chute into the air stream. I saw the pilot chute disappear behind me!

Shit. I couldn't even see the darn thing. I strained my neck, nothing. I dipped my right shoulder, nothing. I looked down and I was over the canal. I counted a few seconds. Double crap! Time for the reserve. Of course, I remembered that with no bag or main visible, I should cut it away. So I cut away and remembered to keep the handle. I pulled the reserve and expected a quick opening.

Nothing. A few seconds went by. And then I remember thinking very calmly: "That was one jump too many."

The canal was now pretty damn close; I was maybe 800 to 900 feet high, and my brain was calm. Not over-revving, not under-revving; I'm just not panicking. Weirdly, I had nothing out there but I was calm.

"This is it," I thought. But I was flustered because I had seen Audrey demonstrate the reserve pilot chute; that spring was very tight and had a lot of power. So why wasn't the reserve out? I thought that perhaps if I tucked in my legs I might "stand" and the relative wind would brush my back and do something. As soon as I did that, the reserve deployed.

But now I thought, where is the main? I could clearly feel behind my back that the bag was not there. I looked around but did not see a falling bag. Oh shit; I'd lost the main. Brand new one, too. And then I did a nice PLF and landed about 50 yards south of the canal. Of course I was happy to be alive, but angry because I had lost my main. I had seen other people cut away and their main or bag were always found near the DZ. So I gathered in the reserve.

Then I found it. The main was still in the bag and attached to the spring of the reserve and tangled with the main pilot chute. Then the situation became clear: the main pilot chute burbled on my back and somehow the bag moved on top of the reserve pilot chute. When I pulled the reserve, its spring barely moved because the bag was sitting on top of it.

So it was a good thing I had cut away (not to mention trying a sitting position to expose my back to the relative wind.)

As I was walking toward the loft, Alan Richter came up to me; I do not think he understood what had just happened. He congratulated me for having opened the reserve, although a bit low (about 500 feet, he calculated.) I explained what I thought had happened and showed him the pilot chute tangle. He opened his eyes pretty wide and said something like it was a good thing I had lived through all that.

Philip de Louraille

How Does a Blind Man Distinguish a Red Light from an Orange Light?

I was filming the night 40-way world record attempts at Perris with Dave Keith back in '83 or '84. I'd only made one other night dive before—a solo out of a C-180 a decade previously.

For years I never jumped with goggles. I don't know why, looking back, but based on prior behavior patterns, perhaps that's not a surprise. But what I desperately needed was glasses, being practically night-blind due to nearsightedness. So I borrowed a pair from a friend.

At 9 p.m. we gathered for the dirt-dive with chem-lites, rotating helmet beacons, and flashlights. Before the first attempt a couple of people spoke out about their being nervous and wondered if it was okay to feel that way. Sammy Ramos or Craig Fronk answered "Absolutely," and we all breathed a collective sigh.

So there we were on jump run two hours later, trundling along at 15 grand in Skip's DC-3, chem-lites fading and moon almost down, with 41 other hypoxic jumpers wondering, "How the fuck did I get talked into this?"

Not me. I was thinking about diving blind with a six-pound brick on my head … and how I was about to die. Would I blow through someone else's open canopy because I arrived too late, or would I take someone still in the formation out in my no-look/no-lift dive? It was settled as far as I was concerned. The only other unresolved issue was whether it would make the next day's newspaper or the following day.

Dave and I had discussed our break-off. We decided the safe bet was that since it would be a little crazy at break-off, and since neither of us wanted to track blind, we could take advantage of our camera slots. We would pull as the formation broke. I would get on the side of the formation where the guy in the base had an orange beacon on his helmet (or was it red?) and Dave would get behind the guy on the opposing side. His light was red (or was it orange?)

Question: How does a blind man distinguish a red light from an orange light—especially when he forgets which color is his?

Answer: He doesn't.

Amazingly, I finally got right above the formation. Those of you who have exited last out of a DC-3 with 42 on board, tell me what you see when your knees finally hit the breeze? Correct … Nothing. Now tell me what a blind man sees when doing the same exit at night?

Going camera, I never became good at diving and I had to somehow find this formation, standing on my head (which had a giant piece of aluminum strapped to it.) I could barely do this during daylight hours, but at night? I dove and I dove and I dove. No formation. So I kept diving. Then, suddenly it appeared. It had built to about 30 by the time I got down to it. Suddenly it lit up—as if lightning had struck! It happened again! Then again!

It was Dave Keith's strobe going off and for a moment I was stunned. I never imagined, in all my preparation, what this was going to look like. It was stunning. Blackness pierced by a barrage of strobe flashes from both his camera and mine. First nothing—then, in an instant a 36-way appeared! Bang! Bang! Bang! Bang! Bang! (You can see the photo on my Facebook page.) It was breathtaking! But no sooner had I reached the formation than it was time to go.

Now came the decision. In my haste to get down to the formation, I had forgotten which light I was supposed to line up behind. Did it matter anyway, being half-blind? I could see the flash from Dave's strobe, but I couldn't see Dave. Where was he? I had this awful feeling when my pilot chute left my hand.

When we landed, I saw Dave. He walked over to me and with the calmest, softest voice asked, "Do you know where I was?"

I told him that I had a strong premonition that I was about to find out. He said, without any anger, "If it wasn't for the fact that your pilot chute went just past my right cheek, you and I wouldn't be standing here now. As soon as I saw it, I barrel-rolled to get out of your way."

Randy Forbes

Slow and Methodical

We were doing a big-way over Perris in the late '70s. When it came time to open I tracked away, looking for an open space to deploy. I dumped my PC and no shit, it malfunctioned.

I pulled the covers down on my Capewells, yanked down on both, and fell away from the garbage. Being the experienced skydiver that I was, I didn't look at my reserve ripcord when I came in to pull. Of course, I missed it. I looked down to get a visual, put my hand on it, and pulled. By the time I actually pulled, however, I went head-down and my R-2 Piglet reserve hit my foot and wrapped around it.

I remember seeing others from the group go by and I looked down at the ground. I was head-down, with a horseshoed reserve.

Okay, I'm thinking this was it. I was going to die. I looked up at my foot and thought I might be able to push the mess off with my other foot. So I slowly and methodically started to push the canopy off my foot. My reserve finally opened and I had an uneventful ride down.

When I gathered in my reserve and was heading back, Doo-Dah (Keith Hendricks) started walking with me. I asked him if he saw me, and he said, "Ya, you went by me and you were kicking like a muther."

So much for being slow and methodical.

Bob Celaya

Maybe I Should Open In This Cloud

I think this was in November or December of 1984. A few of us wanted to form a team to go to the Nationals in 1985 and compete in 4- and 8-way. This was just for fun and experience. We were nowhere close in skills to Visions, a team that jumped every weekend.

It could have been our third or fourth week together. The weather that day was cloudy but there were holes in the clouds, so up we went in the Skyvan.

As we were nearing 12,500 feet, we couldn't see the DZ. There was partial cloud cover below. The pilot went around once, and then again. There were still no cloud openings, but via radio the DZ told him that the clouds were high, well above 3,500 feet. So he told us he had this directional instrument and knew when we would be over the DZ. He told us to just jump when he said "Go" and we'd open over the DZ.

I was not overly happy with this plan, but I was not the only one on the team. Our captain, Bill Baker, wanted us to jump. He said we'd all be fine ... blah blah blah. Okay, so we lined up and waited for the pilot's signal. He was watching the instrument panel, and finally he said, "Go, go, go, now, go, go, NOW!" and out the door we went.

We did our thing (not a terribly successful dive as I recall) and went through a cloud or two. When it was break-off time at 3,500 feet, there were clouds just below us. I remember my instructors five years earlier telling us that we should not open in a cloud as we could collide with another jumper. So I went through the clouds, noticing that two or three of my teammates had opened above the clouds; the rest of us were still tracking away.

I tracked until 2,000 feet, and was still in the clouds. I tracked some more, and then a few seconds later I decided to open the main. The hell with that rule.

My chute opened nicely, I got my toggles in my hands, then looked down and ... *Holy Shit!* I was about to land in some hills, or what looked like hills. I could barely discern the terrain from the cloud or fog I was in. So there I landed, wondering where the hell I was or why hills grew on the DZ while we were up there. Holy crap ... had I waited one or two more seconds, I would have gone in.

So I packed my chute on the wet grassy spot I landed on and started down the slope, hoping to find a road or something. None of my teammates were nearby.

About 15 minutes later I saw Gayle Baker and Karen; they were jumping for joy and gave me a nice hug as they were crying. Through their sobs I understood that they thought I had bounced. I was the last one to open (they saw that) and my teammates landed a few seconds after opening, too. Five minutes earlier they had encountered a log of wood on their way down the hill, and through the fog they had thought at first that it was my body.

Fortunately, the hills were steep so I had missed the top where they had landed.

We finally all got together and realized we had jumped over the hills near Quail Valley—between Perris and Elsinore. The difference in ground altitude between the drop zone and the hills was about 1,500 feet.

We found our way back to the DZ (and the rest of the team on the way.) We were pissed at the pilot for insisting we go when he said so, and we were nowhere near the DZ. We were more like six or seven miles south of it.

After we dumped our gear on the ground and told Dick *(Giarrusso, DZ manager)* what had happened, he called the pilot over and started giving him a few choice words. The pilot said something like "Yeah, yeah, yeah" with a very casual attitude. Dick punched him in the stomach and knocked the wind out of him. Then he told him: "Now that I have your attention: Never ever tell my jumpers when to jump. Understood?"

Philip de Louraille

Flat On My Back at a Thousand Feet

July 19th, 1980: Chambersburg Municipal Airport, also known as the Southern Cross Drop Zone.

The sky was blue, and the breeze was perfect. Larry was about to make his 500th jump, so we all wanted to do something cool. There were ten of us on the load, but typical 10-ways seemed too mundane.

One of my favorite scenes on film was from *"Wings,"* Carl Boenish's film with the sequential diamond dive where the center man pulls out of the formation. So we decided on a nine-way diamond with me on the point as a stinger, looking back at the diamond and shooting Super-8 film.

We loaded into George's AN-2 and headed into the blue. At 8,500 feet we turned on jump run. The green light came on and I slipped into the rear floater spot.

Off we went. I was shooting the exit string, watching that big gray biplane getting smaller and smaller. I was pinned by the diamond point man before the last man hit the prop blast. The diamond built so quickly and smoothly that I was envisioning in my brain a scene that would rival Carl's film.

At 4,500 feet I gave Larry the nod and in the midst of eight screaming, tongue-wagging geekers, he threw out his pilot chute. The burble slowed his deployment a bit, but as he was extracted from the formation, I craned my neck upward to catch his opening sequence.

When we hit 3,500 feet my Paralert began beeping; we all broke off and began to track. Before the beeping stopped, I looked over my right shoulder before waving off. That's when I saw Keith, tracking as hard as he could to catch me (he knew where the camera was)—with his tongue flapping and screaming so loudly that I could actually hear him.

I thought *Okay, this will make for a cool shot* so I kind of rolled onto my left side to film his opening. This movie just kept getting better and better.

By now the beeping had stopped, but I was focused on getting the shot. *Okay Keith, get it out. Um, okay Keith, throw it out already.*

Finally he tossed his pilot chute and I rolled onto my back to record his opening shock. This is the point where I could say in all truthfulness, "There I was, flat on my back at a thousand feet!"

The real shock came when I flipped back onto my belly. I immediately reached back and threw my pilot chute as hard as I could *(wrong canopy)*. Luckily, my opening was crisp, clean and fast. I checked my altimeter—just a tick below 600 feet.

I landed way out, which gave me lots of time to think about what had just happened. Each time I rehashed the jump in my mind, the scarier it got. That jump could very well have been my last.

The good news was that George was busy in the hangar and didn't see any of this, so I never got grounded. The bad news was that I discovered a broken wire on the battery pack for my camera, and not one second of this awesome dive was captured on film.

Dean Widerman

I'm Still Alive

It was the 15th of September 1968, my jump number was 482, and I had just broken out of a five-way star with Jim Bohr, Joan Schlee, Jerry Halvaka, and Dana Parker at Hinckley. I was in a full track and happier than a pig in the mud as it was the DZ's first five-way.

Nearing a grand, I sat up and pulled. I was wearing a piggyback with a PC and a 26-foot steerable conical. When I should have felt opening shock, I looked up and saw a beautiful streamer. As I reached for the Capewells, I looked at the ground rushing up and having made several intentional cutaways, I knew how unreliable they were.

Safety and survival flashed thru my drug-crazed brain. I grabbed my reserve ripcord handle and pulled. I waited for either opening shock or the ground to hit. They weren't far apart.

The reserve opening shock was brutal. I thought to myself *Oh my god, I hit the fucking ground*. But I hadn't.

I reached up and grabbed the reserve's steering toggles as I looked down. I landed in the middle of a small shallow creek. I stood there in water up to my knees, rubbing my riser burned neck and contemplating my near brush with death when Jim Peterson, also known as Twink, and Louie Jecker ran up screaming profanities at me and calling me a dumb fuck for not cutting away. All I could say was "Hey, I'm still alive."

Nearly three years later at the Rainbow DZ in Franklin, Wisconsin, I found myself in the same situation. I was going through a grand with another streamer. I did the same thing: reached up and pulled my reserve ripcord handle. As it was dusk and I was low and out of the landing area, no one saw me open or land. On the walk back I promised myself I would start pulling a little higher.

FEDO (Robert Federman)

Focused On Landing Alive

One cloudy day at CG Wallace's DZ in Crosby, Texas, a civilian restaurant owner invited us to drop in: "Hey, y'all come fly on over where you boys can parachute here into my place. The folks will love it and I'll give you all free eats, too."

So five of us loaded up in the Cessna 195, climbed to just below the clouds at about 1,600 feet, and threw three streamers to plot the exit at about 1,500 feet for the free-food demo.

Carlos spotted. Everybody did a fairly long delay except for me. We all exited with our floating ripcords in hand. Me, a turkey, arched a bit and popped my main just off the step. Ouch! Embarrassing! I was open above a grand.

Nobody noticed my opening, however, as this was a small restaurant with a not-so-big parking lot. Lots of cars were there, too. It was real easy to get focused on landing alive.

At about 200 feet Carlos got freaked by all the obstacles and landed on the restaurant's roof. Skippy Mannino, thinking that this was way cool, did the same. The rest of us landed among the parked cars. I did a messy front-roll PLF.

The restaurant owner was way impressed, saying something like, "Amazing, wonderful, great that you two fellows could actually land on my roof! Who would have thunk? 'Course, I'm certain you boys don't know that your landing knocked our ceiling fluorescent light tubes smack onto my tables, customers, and food. So, I'm gonna have to close down for a spell and clean things up. Real sorry about that. But you men come on back by here some other time and I'll give you that free lunch like I promised."

While Carlos took the heat, the rest of us decided to get some beer and slink back to the DZ. It was too cloudy to jump anyway.

Pat Works

It Was Fun Until He Got the Plane's Nose Down

Sometime in late 1972, five of us decided to squeeze into a C-180 at the Mooresville DZ in Indiana. I volunteered to shimmy along to hang all the way out on the strut. Another grabbed the strut while keeping his feet on the wheel, while another swung to the prop-side of the strut and so on until one person was left in the door. It took a little time to get everyone in position, and the pilot was careful to slow his airspeed to accommodate us.

Maybe a little too careful, because just as we started the count the plane stalled and the right wing dropped straight down with me still hanging on.

Everybody else fell away, but I decided to hang on because of what I had learned when I was a student pilot. Please correct me if this is inaccurate, but I remember practicing dynamic (or "wing-over") stalls. The first thing that you must do when the right wing drops is to push the nose down and immediately apply more power to regain airspeed.

At least that was what I anticipated the pilot was going to do. If I dropped away and the pilot executed a proper stall recovery, I would be at risk of a prop strike if the plane caught up with me. Not a pleasant thought. So I hung on and went for the ride of my life!

It was fun until he got the plane's nose down. As I continued to hang on, I noticed that my body position did not resemble a flag or a streamer. Instead it stayed the same relative to the ground, so that I was still hanging straight down, but now the nose along with the prop had swung down and around beside me, with the plane's nose going straight down.

I couldn't let go if I wanted to. If I had dropped away at that point the prop, which was now spinning next to me only a few feet away, could have easily caught up to me and struck me, so I hung on, like a bastard, until the pilot gained enough airspeed to pull it out.

Once he gained control and started to pull the nose up, I just let go. I never got to the formation.

Randy Forbes

We Want Our Entry Fees Back

Notwithstanding our team's status as hero-hopefuls, fate conspired against us. Our eye-opening near-death religious experience with the ground happened on our second 10-man jump at a big Rumbleseat Trophy Competition jump a long time ago—sometime in the mid-1970s.

After a good exit, D-Ray went low on the formation. It was a mere stumble—so okay, we'll wait for him to float up and close. Being committed team players, all of us held in place. Nine of us in the star patiently took it through 1,500 feet. Awed and proud, I knew we were low. But I was astounded that all of us were still waiting for D-Ray's entry, unflinching and in-formation. Half of these stalwarts had never opened below two grand—and they were still in freefall. We waited and waited and …waited.

I was impressed. Team spirit! I got a lump in my throat at our hanging in there. Togetherness! A solid Rock of Gibraltar. Gee!

D-Ray looked down. Then he looked up at us. D-Ray looked down again, shook his head as in *"no way"*, waved off, and pulled. I promptly pulled right out of the formation. Our White Hat mates turned 180 degrees to track! Wow! Remarkable—but not too swift—given the lurking ground. They zoomed away to get open at about 600 to 800 feet.

Eek! Freak-out terror! Many were all tense and twitchy in their after-landing rush. Bill Davis was low man at 400 feet; Bob Butt was less than a grand…again. Never-low Greg Burrows was at 600 feet.

There were four ground judges on telemeters watching this madness. An emotional judge came over and informed us, "Wow! You guys were so close I had to look away from the telemeters to see if you got the formation or not."

Although it is not difficult to comprehend today, the judges threw us out of the meet. We were contrite, sort of. Dirty Ed was pissed, very. He marched right up to the judges and puffed up like a toad to complain. But the judges were adamant: "You are outta here!"

Ed reared up and roared, "You can't throw us out of the meet. We resign! We want our entry fees back."

Ed had impressive volume; we got our entry fees back. Then we had some serious safety meetings in my van to consider the cause and corrective action of this indiscreet jump.

I forget what we said. But I still recall that competition day was a pretty one. Nice spring day. Lots of sunshine. No clouds. Big time 10-way parachute meet! Jerry Bird's team won. There was a good party later.

Pat Works

An Altimeter and Compass

It was April 12, 1969. NSTIWTIWGD.

After a day's jumping at Taft, Don "Bucky" Bucktel and I flew with Lyle Cameron in his Stinson Mule V-77 from Taft to Lakeside. We didn't have any running lights or radio so I could see right away how things were going to go on this trip. I think we only had an altimeter and compass.

As we got close to the Ridge Route the clouds started to close in on us. We turned SSW to see if we could spot car lights below through the clouds so we could follow them up and over the pass at Gorman. It turned out we were not even over the Ridge Route. We were going up a canyon just to the west of it. We found this out when we broke out of the clouds and Lyle yelled, *"Oh shit!"*—then turned us on our side and did a fast 180 to go back up north to the valley.

We figured out where we were and tried again. This time we were over the Ridge Route and we made it to the San Fernando Valley. We then turned southeast and headed in the direction of Hollywood.

Lyle flew the Mule down Hollywood Boulevard and, although not wearing a rig, Bucky got out on the step and started yelling at people walking down the sidewalk. Lyle told me to get Bucky's ass back inside because we had a headwind and Bucky was dragging us down. I think we were maxed out at about 45 mph at the time.

We had to make a few stops on the way to pick up fuel to feed that beast. One stop was at Oceanside where we siphoned enough fuel from planes that were tied down to get us a few miles over to Palomar. I don't know where he got them, but Lyle came back with some bulbs for the running lights. When we got to Palomar late that night, Lyle called a friend of his who worked the tower there to come back to the airport and fill up the Mule.

With no radio, we had to wait for a green light from the little tower to take off. On rotation Lyle proceeded to turn and do a very slow buzz-job on the tower. I watched as the green light in the tower went down to the floor.

As I remember it, I think the Mule crashed at Perris a few years later. A jumper got hung up on the tail and went in with it. Bill Shearer was flying it and he made it out just as the wing folded; the strut came in and hit his head on exit.

Dennis Henley

Dumping Just Slightly Above the Beer Can Dump

By the mid-1960s Security had invented the convertible harness and container system with which you could move the belly wart and make it a piggyback. And that was the beginning of this NSTIWTIWGD story.

Lyle Cameron, the famous editor of *Sky Diver* magazine and one of the cameramen on the old *Ripcord* TV show, was my civilian Sky Daddy. He asked me to "test hop" one of those Security convertible rigs. All you had to do was unzip the reserve, move it from back to front, and reposition the main container. The 26-foot conical reserve was attached with military Koch fittings and had the conventional half-inch tubular nylon cross-connector on the risers as a standard safety feature.

After riding my 1961 BMW R69S to the Lakeside DZ, I quickly hooked up the Koch fittings on the piggyback configuration, reattached the bungees, tossed the rig on a packing table, and headed toward manifest.

Louie and Eddie Melendez had come down from LA and we planned a three-way from 7,500 feet. Without a gear check, I scooped up my rig and ran for the Cessna.

I'll cut right to the good parts of this story. We were passing through three grand and Eddie was fumbling for his floating ripcord handle. Lou and I were close in, watching and laughing. Eddie finally dumped; Lou paused, then dumped, and I went to pull a skosh under two thousand feet.

But I couldn't pull the damn ripcord with one hand! Now I had both hands on the D-ring and I was tugging real hard. Still, there was nothing. That ripcord wasn't going to budge even if I put a foot in it. I swear I could read the labels in the beer can dump next to the runway as I passed through a grand. I stood up, pulled the reserve, and felt it coming off my back.

Then it all turned into a WTF moment. The reserve sniveled a little, I was getting ground rush, the conical was finally in the breeze, and I got opening shock. I was hanging by only one riser. The Koch fitting on one side had become undone (or maybe I just hadn't attached it in the first place.)

I was probably 500 feet or lower, and I had one riser about a foot higher than my other. Thankfully, the cross-connector strap was holding and I had a pretty full canopy, but I noticed the strap had almost burned through.

My reserve was augering (corkscrewing) in tight circles, and I was trying to get the main out, too—anything to get me into a feet-first landing attitude. A couple of seconds later I landed hard on the dirt runway next to the beer can dump, miraculously unharmed.

The comedy in all this was Loretta Breese screaming at her husband (the DZO): "Vance, Vance! Chip Maury is having another low-pull contest. Ground that sonofabitch!"

I got another rig and made a couple more jumps before deploying back to Vietnam a couple of weeks later.

I forgot to mention why I couldn't pull. The top of the first pin locked on the mouth of the twisted (90 degrees, we found out later) ripcord housing. There was no plate securing the end to the container. We repacked the main and tried to pull it, but there was no way to dump when the pin got stuck. Seeing the nylon-on-nylon burn almost all the way through the half-inch tubular gave me a greater "pucker factor" than moments before augering in. If that had parted, there would have been no chance of survival.

The Good Lord protects fools, drunks and sailors! Also Cardinals, Supreme Cardinals, Bishops and Popes, too.

Security fixed that problem real fast.

Chip Maury

I Could See the Whites of Their Eyes

The time was the early 1970s; the place: Skylark Field on a dark and overcast day. We jumpers were startled by the noisy arrival of a WWII trainer, a T-17 Valiant (think T-6, but with fixed gear.) Everyone swarmed the aircraft, but somehow I was the one who talked the pilot into letting me jump it!

I assumed that the pilot would take me up and return for his passenger, but noooo. He said: "I'll just remove the stick in the rear cockpit; plenty of room."

So I geared up and squeezed in, sorta kneeling/squatting on the floor between the passenger's knees. (It's a good thing I was a very skinny kid and that I had my very first piggyback rig.)

I had explained to the pilot over and over that I needed at least 2,500 feet *above ground level*. So, I was a bit surprised when we turned in on jump-run and I looked down to see all my friends out at the peas and I could recognize individual faces. I motioned to the pilot in the front cockpit and he tapped his altimeter and shouted over the drone, "Hell, I gotcha almost three thousand feet!"

The aircraft altimeter indicated around 2,950 feet. Elsinore is about 1,250 feet above sea level (you do the math.) I shouted and gestured "More altitude, *more altitude!!*" But the pilot just smiled and indicated, "Yeah, thumbs-up to you, too, Buddy!"

I looked down and could see people waving and smiling; hell, I could see their *eyes* … and I hadn't left the plane yet! I managed to stand up and get one foot up on the window railing. I took one last look at my very-close friends down below, and then fixated on the horizontal stabilizer. It was the size of a barn door and very, very close to the rear cockpit.

I took a firm grip on my reserve handle, hoping that if I hit the tail I would fire it instinctively. Then I jumped down and out as hard as I could. Suddenly it got very quiet as I fell away from that lumbering radial engine. I realized that I had survived the exit, so I quickly dumped my round main and, after a *(ahem)* somewhat brief canopy ride, I landed in the peas to the cheers of the throng and my friends' shouts of "Beer, case of beer!"

The DZ's management couldn't even ground me—because it wasn't a low pull, it was a low exit!

Those were the days, my friend; those were the days!

Jerry Swovelin

Jumpmaster In-Tow Over Texas

A "jumper in-tow" means that a jumper is hung up on the aircraft and cannot separate on his own. Many years ago, the most common cause of this uncommon event was a static line that did not release. Normally, it was the student who (with pin-type static line) got suspended below the jump ship, requiring knives, carabiners and heroics to solve the problem. The jumpmaster's challenge was to save both student and aircraft, and avoid littering the area with parts of either.

In the dim daze of yesteryear—about 1965—at Wallace's DZ, there is the true story of our jumpmaster, Mr. One-Ear Brumley.

One-Ear Brumley was a Houston fireman. I dunno how he lost his ear. We jumped a Cessna 195/196. The Pilot was Rufus Ramsey, the Round Weed Roller. Except for the participants, it was a sort of normal jump. There was one static-line student. A first-timer, she was a butt-ugly fat chick. Also on the load were her jumpmaster (One-Ear) and three other skydivers who'd planned a four-way with One-Ear.

On the low pass jump-run, the student Butt-Ugly (aka BU) refused to exit. Froze up. Nope, was not going to leave; no-way, no how. Being too big to just kick in the head and encourage out, BU was relocated behind the pilot for the high pass.

At 7,500 feet (a normal high-altitude pass in those days) the skydivers exited. Except for Jumpmaster One-Ear. One-Ear hung below the Cessna kicking and screaming a bit. Rufus Ramsey, the Round Weed Roller and Pilot, leaned out the door and noticed One-Ear; they had some sort of a discussion. It seemed that On-Ear was caught by the foot and hung from the aircraft's step (which was shaped like an "L".) The tongue of the step somehow got stuck up One-Ear's cowboy boot.

Rufus Ramsey, the Round Weed Roller, did some aerobatics—wiggling the plane and such. One-Ear accompanied him with what might have been Wagnerian Opera. BU was crying and discussing her family. This went on for way too long, as the story was told to me, and included several passes over the airport's grass strip. Brumley could sing way loud.

Finally, Rufus Ramsey, the Round Weed Roller, got BU to switch places with him… *"Just hold it straight and steady … I will return in a jiffy … just be a moment …"* Rufus then hung himself out the open door and wrestled with One-Ear, the wind, the cowboy boot, and lady luck. Since Rufus was not wearing his parachute, the spectators on the ground were rooting for Rufus. Rufus won. The boot came off. One-Ear hitchhiked back to the DZ, arriving about 45 minutes after the airplane landed.

On landing, BU exclaimed to the world in general her current feelings about the sport. (They were not real positive at all). She was called a heroine, One-Ear's savior, a budding pilot, a wonderful person, etc. (We only had the one airplane and pilots were hard to find.) She quickly asserted that the hero stuff was all B/S. Big- eyed, like the wheel is spinning, but the hamster is dead.

Said she: "I did NOT fly any airplane … never! That man (Rufus Ramsey, the Round Weed Roller) forced me into that tiny seat! The steering wheel thing was squished against my bosoms (and chest-mounted reserve) ... I could not have drove that airplane to save my life."

About then, One-Ear arrived back from the near-dead. His faith renewed, he proclaimed his undying love and respect for Butt-Ugly and proposed marriage as heartfelt thanks. Lord love a duck, they did marry.

The cowboy boot was never found.

Pat Works

I Had to Pull at 4,500 Feet

NSTIWTIWGD … It all started back in 1966 on my thirteenth jump, from 7,500 feet by myself—it was a 30-second normal jump on which I encountered stability problems, a flat spin. I went into a head-down dive to correct it, and when I got to 1,000 feet I pulled, got open at about 750-800 feet, and I liked it!

That's where it all started. From time to time I was clocked way below this altitude, so this story probably won't come as a surprise to you.

Most of you are familiar with Gary Douris (RIP). He bought a stopwatch that only went to one minute just to clock my time under canopy. What's up with that? I have been grounded at least three or four times at most DZs, and lots more at Elsinore for pulling low. This is just to let you know I pulled low most of the time. I know some of you remember.

It was a beautiful day out at Elsinore in 1973. We were team practicing for the Nationals, and had just made a 10-man star that we took down to … well, let's just say a little below 1,800 feet where we broke it off. This was so you could get a good look at it from the ground. Guess what? Larry Perkins was standing right below us and watched the whole thing. To make a long story short, Al and Larry went into the hangar to work something out so we could continue jumping and go to the Nationals. Al came out and said we had to agree to a few things.

First, we would get one thousand feet more altitude than we paid for, but everyone had to be open before 2,000 feet. AGL.

Secondly, anyone jumping with us who opened below 2,000 feet would get the whole team grounded for a 30-day period. Now comes the bad part.

The third condition was that Bud (that would be me) had to pull at 4,500 feet.

I talked as fast as I could against this as everyone knows an RW canopy won't open above 2,500 feet. At that altitude there isn't enough oxygen to keep you alive. Yes, I tried all the excuses. None of them worked, and at that moment in time, my life as a dirty low puller was coming to an end.

If you are still reading, here it comes: the NSTIWTIWGD story that will make that three-seconds-from-death story that Tim Long shared with us sound like an eternity.

I was hornswoggled. We packed up and got on the next load. At 11,500 feet, our exit went well; we built a clean 10-man, and here came 4,500 feet. Yes, I pulled and that's when everything went bad. I had a malfunction—spinning, no less. I opened the Capewell covers (I had shot-and-a-halfs,) put my thumbs through the loops and pulled, expecting that mess to go away.

It didn't. I pulled at the left, then the right, then both again and again, going through 4,000 … 3,500 … 3,000 feet. I heard *"Cut away, cut away!"* (I wish I would have thought of that) as I went through 2,500 feet. As I'm thinking *"This can't end in anything good,"* just below 2,000 feet *Click!* the right riser released. Not good; now I started spinning even faster.

"Cheer up," I thought, *"things could be worse,"* so I cheered up and sure enough, things got worse.

Now pushing 1,000 feet, it wasn't looking good … 900 … 800 … 700 feet. At 500 feet, I know it will be time to dump my reserve even if I can't get rid of this rag. Here it comes: 500 feet. Bend over and kiss your ass goodbye because spinning this fast, there is no way the reserve has a chance of opening.

All this time I was still pulling on that Capewell, trying to get it to release. Going through 500 feet, I gave it one more pull, knowing full well that the next pull would be my reserve handle, with or without that damn main canopy. I wasn't going to go in with one good parachute on my back. *SNAP!* the left riser released. I knew I was only a couple of seconds from the ground. As the riser and I parted company, it was followed very closely by my reserve pilot chute.

I could feel each stow band releasing … *thump, thump* … one at a time. It seemed like forever until the crack of that reserve opening. It hurt so good. I had plenty of time to reach up and grab the risers before I hit the ground. I was open a good 30 to 40 feet above the ground. I don't know why I was starting to panic; I've had lower openings at the river.

Oh well, NO SHIT THERE I WAS THOUGHT I WAS GOING TO DIE. I can say this got me thinking maybe there is something to this 2,000-ft. opening altitude idea, and I would like to thank Larry Perkins and Al Krueger for saving my life. If they hadn't made me pull at 4,500 feet, it would have been a dirt dive. Thanks for reading this.

Walther Spasuzi (aka Bud Krueger)

Cut Away, Larry, Cut Away

I was doing my 18th jump in June 1971 over Kinnet, Missouri. It was a demo. I spotted a three-way over downtown Kinnet and exited at 7,500 feet. After the formation I tracked, waved off, and started the deployment sequence. At 2,500 feet I had a fully opened Para-Commander in the new psychedelic color.

Until, that is, I initiated a turn to downwind toward the target. Then I heard *"Clink"* and my right riser disconnected, producing a streamer. Training, fear, and adrenaline kicked in to produce a verbal command: *"Cut away, Larry, cut away!"*

I cut away and had a semi-stable deployment of my reserve, producing a good canopy. Now I was under 2,000 feet and dead center over downtown Kinnet. But my maneuverability was limited and the wind was not as strong as it was on take-off. Running hard to the landing area, realizing I was not going to make it, I noticed the fairgrounds arena as my only option and turned to run for it.

It looked like I was going to make it until I saw the power lines hanging between two light poles. NSTIWTIWGD!

I cleared the power lines by lifting my legs; then I yanked a low turn and landed in left-over horse shit in the middle of the arena.

Malfunction cause: an improperly locked one-and-a-half-shot capewell on a demo PC that was switched into the container at the last minute. My jumpmaster, Ron Carter, missed it on the safety check. His explanation: "Sorry I missed that capewell. So, do you want to buy the PC?"

I said, "Fuck you!"

Larry Frankenbach

I'm OK

On April 30, 1977, I rode over to Perris from Elsinore with Mary Wolfrank. The *Fallin' Angels* female skydivers were going to do a demo at the annual Chino Fly-In at the Chino Airport. Mary told me that she had cut her hand the night before. It was sore, so she did not snap her main shut and only used the Velcro to close it.

Eleven of us loaded a D-18 at the Perris Valley Airport. It was piloted by Bob Jones, aka BJ. BJ had only one eye, so depth perception was not his strong point.

Mary was spotting and going rear floater. I was following her out as front floater. After the cut she started to climb out and instantly disappeared. I looked out the door; she was hanging off the rear stabilizer, her main over the top of it, her helmet (and head) under. In the meantime, everyone else thought that Mary was in freefall and were pushing to get out the door. I did my best to keep them from exiting. My thought was, *If Mary isn't okay, at least we have 10 more chances to help her off the plane.* Then she looked at me, mouthed "I'm OK," and cut away. She opened her reserve shortly thereafter.

Even though everybody was pretty shook up, we felt the show must go on. Sally Miller came back to the rear of the plane to spot. She and BJ were doing a good job lining us up over the airport. She was about to yell for a cut when I looked out and saw great big airplanes sitting on the tarmac. We were over nearby Ontario International Airport.

I yelled "Ninety right." We waited a few minutes and were over Chino again. The rest of the jump went off without any problems and we made a nice star. M. Anderson Jenkins went last so he could film us.

The rest of the ladies on the load were Jan Works, JoAnn Nelson, Wendy Neustrup, Chris Doss, Cherrie Kinley, Marilyn Perrine, Sally Miller and Carol Dekeyser. Pam Gigante was on the ground announcing and from what I heard, she did such a nice job that the crowd was unaware of the drama happening at 12,500 feet and didn't realize that Mary's reserve ride wasn't supposed to be part of the show.

After we landed, BJ did a buzz job. I don't think he had a clue how badly damaged the stabilizer was. At any rate, he landed the D-18 safely back at Perris. The legendary Tiny Broadwick had been the special guest at the airshow and joined us back at Cherrie Kinley's house later that day.

Shari Schmidt

Only Bird Shit and Fools Fall From the Sky

In May 1979 I had just finished two years at the University of Maine. I was majoring in skydiving, with drinking for my minor and whoring as an elective. Once in a while I went to class. A $2,500 student loan bought a lot of jumps and beer back then.

I was a 200-jump wonder, cocky as bantam rooster, and invincible. I had just scored a brand new Wonderhog, Strong Lo-Po reserve, and a Cruisair from the regional Pepsi distributor. The Pepsi logo covered the entire bottom of the canopy. It was mine to keep. All I had to do was make about a dozen demos for them for two years. They'd send the plane and I'd select my buddies for the jumps. We'd do the dives, get dinner (on Pepsi) and they'd send us home with five or six cases of beer. (They were a Heineken distributor as well.)

I was still waiting for my new gear at semester's end when I went up to Houlton, Maine, to jump with some of my original instructors and friends. I had been to Pelicanland and Z-Hills, handled a total malfunction, and by Jesus, I was a Sky God. Just ask me!

The Houlton airport is huge and surrounded by potato fields. It was a mile away from the Canadian border. You could throw a blind person out under a non-steerable chute and they would still land on the airport. We used to go to 10,500 feet in an old Cessna 172, get out over Canada, and track back to the U.S.

This particular day gave us no more than 6,000 feet and the winds were blowing harder than a load of coke going up Keith Richards' nose.

I made a jump with my old instructor and another friend, a three-way from 5,000 feet. I spotted long and backed into the packing area under my short-lined Papillion that had so many burn holes it looked like it had been jumped through the finale of a fireworks display. At the time I figured, *Screw the winds; just spot long and I'd be all set.*

I was soon to learn otherwise. Second load it was me, Lyman Pryor, and an observer. Lyman and I went out, did a two-way, and rode it down to 2,500 feet where I did a pull-off. I watched it go and got a pansy-assed opening shock. That was my first clue. It looked like someone had tied the whole right hand side of that parachute into granny knots.

I grabbed the shot-and-a-halfs and chopped it. The old White Angel came off my chest. I remember saying to myself, *Way to go Zeko, Slicker 'n Shit!* I grabbed the red-marked steering lines and turned toward the landing area. That's when I knew it wasn't going to be a good day. At the end of the airport was a sawmill with electrical lines that looked like they carried some serious voltage, and they sure as Hell did! The power lines were on all four sides of the sawmill, and stacked about four feet high for a total of six on each side.

Two years earlier I had watched from the plane as a student hit those things. I saw a big flash and a puff of smoke. Everyone thought she had bought the farm. Fortunately she didn't touch any of the wires, lived to land on the hangar roof the following weekend, and fell 30 feet onto the tarmac when the wind inflated her canopy and dragged her off. One of the guys told her to try bingo. She had 15 jumps and every one of them was a disaster. I called her Daisy Death.

The wind was driving me right toward the same "barbecue pit." I turned back into the wind which was about as useless as teats on a tomcat, and looked over my shoulder. At the rate I was going I figured I'd hit the top tier of the lines straight on, about in the middle of my chest. I could already smell the smoke and my burning carcass. I hoped they would break it gently to my mother. My father's proclamation that *"Only bird shit and fools fall from the sky"* had significant meaning right about then.

I grabbed as many of the front lines as I could in each hand and pulled to beat Hell. It helped burn some altitude, but I was still gonna fry!

I made it over the first set of wires and was coming up on the neatly stacked piles of lumber in the center of that elevated electric chair. They were 12 feet high and there was about a foot of space between each pile.

Suddenly there was lull in the wind. I still was trying to roll the nose up when I looked straight down at the lumber right beneath me. It was coming up fast. I realized that the worst I was going to get out of this cluster-fuck was a mangled leg; about that time I landed square on top of a pile, slid on my ass, and stood up.

There were about two dozen jumpers, hangar rats and assorted rubberneckers coming toward me as I stood reveling in my new-found humility. I got off lightly with a sprained ankle. Hell of way to learn that you ain't no Sky God, and realize that you have a lot to learn.

That incident made for a good après jump story around the fire, especially when I was stoked with beer. The logbook entry for that jump centered on humility, wisdom and common sense gained the hard way.

Bob Lane

Last Load … Something Was Odd

Serendipity Sunday … the last load.

Something was odd; everyone started tracking away early. Then I saw why. We had arranged that they would pop red smoke on the ground if we were to abort the jump, and there it was. I immediately saw why—the smoke was blowing toward us and we were way downwind.

I figured I would open high. Either I would have enough air to get me back, or at least to find someplace safe to land. Well, not only had the wind turned 180 degrees, it had gained another 10 knots.

Like an elevator to Hell, I was going straight down. With the extra altitude I had plenty of time to see there was nothing but suburbs below. Not even a parking lot—just rooftops, roads, and a shit load of telephone lines.

I lined up on one of the longer parallel roads and figured I'd have PLF for the main course with asphalt for dessert. The parked cars were going to make this an accuracy run, or so I thought.

The line across the road was coming up fast. I did a braking turn over the lines that ran parallel with the road and watched them pass under me by about five feet. Then I looked up just in time to see the side of a house coming at me.

The ensuing stall was more of a reflex without thought of consequence. As I lay there with my head ringing and the breath knocked out of me, my first thought was *I think all my bones are intact.*

I slowly dug my way out of my canopy which had settled over me, and there stood the homeowner on his porch, jaw hanging open and cigarette dangling from his hand. His first words were: "I don't believe what just happened."

As for me, realizing that every muscle in my body was starting to hurt as the adrenaline wore off, I nonchalantly asked for a ride back to the riverside. He talked a lot during the ride back, I remember him being very animated. I just kept thinking: *NSTIWTIWGD.*

Jeffrey S Poulliot

Jumping Into A Volcano

It all started at the Z-Hills Turkey Meet. I was eavesdropping on a conversation between Jerry Keker and Dave Williams and heard some key phrases like "rock concert" and "demo". I eased my way into the conversation and found out they were talking about the January First demo jump for the Sunshine Festival, which is held smack dab in the center of Diamond Head Crater in Honolulu, Hawaii. When I found out that much, they had to stop talking for a while and fill me in on who to get in touch with if I should just happen to be in the neighborhood.

When I arrived in Honolulu at two o'clock in the morning on December 30th, I called up Randy Cordes and introduced myself as a visiting jumper who wanted to make the demo into the Volcano. I was warmly invited to their house, called *Toad Manor*, one of the highest houses perched on the cliffs overlooking the city.

They informed me the next day that there wasn't a jump planned for that year due to lack of interest. But with the interest that I showed, and the interest that was generated when I mentioned that it might make for an interesting article in the *RWunderground* newsletter, the demo was planned for New Year's Eve.

Randy, Flip Hollstein and I were going to make the jump the next day, or later on that night (it depends on how you look at it.) Just an hour before we were ready to go to the airport, veteran crater jumper Randy came up with a cold sweat and chills *(really!)* "Rag Man" Frazier took his place on the load.

On the ride up, the plane flew over Pearl Harbor. I saw a ship with the smoke blowing straight up, which suckered me into thinking there were no winds. But there were; they blow over the crater and create the same effect as blowing into an empty coke bottle. Veteran crater jumpers know this and do two things: 1) they jump round canopies, and 2) they stay in the middle of the crater.

I did neither and felt the "crater effect" at about 100 ft. when the swirling gusts hit me sideways and turned my Strato-Star in the same direction with a few cells closed. The landing turned into one of those *"Keep the toggles up and try to hit a clear spot 'cause your ass still has to pass over stuff"* landings.

Flip and Rag Man landed where they were supposed to and I didn't break any bones or take out a bunch of junk by the stage, so we called the demo a success.

Whitey, The King of Boogie (Jim Whiting, RIP)

Mexican Madness with the ParaMatadors in Juchitlan, Jalisco

Here's a great NSTIWTIWGD story by Dirty Billy Bishop. He wrote it in 1976, and I published it in my 1978 book <u>Parachuting: United We Fall</u>.
– Pat Works

It seems invariably that when one first hears stories about Mexico, the listener usually stands there taking in the last gruesome detail and then says something like, "Oh well, that's almost as good as what happened to me in TJ back in '67."

But this one is different—honest!

Mexican Intrigue, that's what it was … Mexican Intrigue. See, there's this guy standing there, grinning and casually telling me I'm going in there and fight the next bull: "But after all, Señor, didn't we just jump into this bullring? Why do we have to fight the Toro?"

Must be because he thinks that if we're skydivers, then we'll make good bullfighters. He hands us another beer. The crowd's cheering for the real matadors is diminishing as we swallow the last foamy dregs. I just toss my bottle into a corner and the gates in front of me open. We walk into the ring amid the renewed cheers and shouts of the crowd.

As we walk we are handed the capes. Thank God the alcohol seeps quickly into the blood in the late afternoon heat. We turn and face the opening where The Bull will appear, and fan out into a "Vee." I shake the cape, more like canvas than the soft flowing material I had expected. The door swings open. The crowd seems to quiet, but perhaps it's only focusing my attention.

The Bull stomps into the ring. First he looks toward us, then around the ring, and immediately right back at us. A quick thought flashes through my mind: *Estamos en Mexico.* I move in on the Bull, shake the cape, and shout, "Toro, aha, Toro!"

I've got his attention now. I steady myself for the first pass. Hey, hey… let's wait just a second. I'm getting way ahead of myself relating this thing to you. Let me start by explaining who we are, and just what the hell a bunch of jumpers are doing in a bullring in Mexico.

We are Rick Hinchman, Efren Perez, "Chepe" Perez, Adan Perez, Alfonso, Dan O'Leary and a cast of a few more whose names I can't pronounce (much less spell) or who I never knew formally, but without whose help it might never have gone down the way it did. The place was a town called Juchitlan, an hour's flying time from Guadalajara, in the state of Jalisco down in Mexico.

I first heard the tales of Juchitlan through an old jump buddy, Rick Hinchman, currently a medical student in Guadalajara. Rick was up in the States on one of his periodic trips north. He was bubbling over with this wild story about a demo into a bullring where the jumpers actually fought a bull after they landed. This sounded like a bit too much to believe, I thought, but I went along as I listened. As Rick continued, it began to sound better, much better. In fact, I could even almost see Hemingway himself sitting there in the stands, a Tequila Sunrise in one hand and his free arm wrapped around a Margarita. Rick went on painting word pictures of the town, the people and the jump. Almost before I realized it, I said, "When do we go?" I had locked myself in. Rick picked it up: "Sometime around Mardi Gras, I'll count on seeing you. I'll send the particulars."

During the few months between September and February, I met with Efren and his brother Adan several times at Elsinore and we began firming up the trip's many particulars, tying up the thousand-and-one loose ends. Finally January drew to an end. Efren and Adan set off on the two-thousand-mile trip by truck. I made it down to Tijuana and boarded an Aeromexico flight to Guadalajara.

Rick and Dan O'Leary, another medical student, met me at the airport armed only with a bottle of Suaza Commemorativo, Mexico's finest liquor or best grade of antifreeze, depending on whether you are man or machine. This was January 31st. The demo was scheduled for the fourth of February, so we had some spare time on our hands. Rick and Dan took it upon themselves to get me acclimatized. We spent the next few hectic days and nights in hard preparation with daily doses of street corner cuisine, rural fiestas, long nights of tequila, dark-eyed muchachas, and not too few Mexican songs sung in Irish brogue.

The evening of February 3rd we met up with Efren and Adan, and for the first time met the rest of our "team." There would be six of us jumping into the ring: Rick, Efren, Adan, "Chepe" Perez (a major in the Mexican Army,) and Alfonso (another Mexican Army officer) and, oh yeah, me. We'd fly in from Guadalajara in a Cessna 206, buzz the town to announce ourselves, then climb to altitude and make two or three passes. Chepe and Alfonso would jump on the first, and the rest of us on the second or third, whatever. Organization and good planning are the keys to a good demo.

We spent the rest of the evening packing, bullshitting, telling jump stories and talking cape technique (a good idea if you would rather get the bull than get the horn.) We ended the evening by producing a bottle of moonshine tequila Rick and I had found back up in the hills the day before. The booze proved to be safe; at least I wasn't blind when morning came.

The morning of the fourth seemed to be one of the longest mornings I had spent since waiting for my Army discharge; afternoon reminded me of waiting to graduate from college, but finally everyone showed up around three o'clock and we headed off for the airport. The adventure had really and finally gotten underway.

We expected to hit Juchitlan about an hour or so before sunset. Since there is really no one to notify in Mexico about when or where you are going to jump, our main concerns at the airport revolved around readying the plane, briefing the pilot (incidentally, he had never flown jumpers before, and probably had never seen any before either,) and wondering if we should stash some beer in our jumpsuits for when we landed.

Standing around in an international airport wearing a jumpsuit and rig is really kind of a laugh, especially when you aren't quite sure what the natives and tourists are saying but you've got a good idea about what they are thinking: *Sorry ma'am, they only give parachutes to passengers in First Class; 'bye now.*

We took off behind a 727 and sat back for the flight, another 50-minute eternity. We came in low over the hills and headed up a long valley. Chepe saw it first. "There's Juchitlan!"

We made several low passes and I got a glimpse of the target. *Christ, you couldn't even get a tennis court in that sucker,* I thought, *and no alternates either.* Rick looked and grinned; then he said, "Told you it was tight, didn't I?"

"No Brown Material," I said.

We climbed and came in on jump-run. Suddenly there were three people spotting. I was next to the pilot and couldn't see anything, so I kept giving him right turns. Chepe turned around and gave a cut. He and Alfonso disappeared out the door. We circled and watched. Both of them went right 'in' perfectly. We were losing daylight and time, so we decided that all four of us—Rick, Efren, Adan, and I—would go on the next pass. Rick and I would do a two-man. We hit four grand and headed in.

Rick spotted. *Cut.* Efren and Adan tumbled out. Rick looked at me like "Well?" and I yelled "Go!"

We rolled out and I looked for Rick to start for the pin. Then I remembered ... the smoke! I reached around and pulled the thing, then looked for Rick, then the ground, again for Rick, then the ground, at the horizon, at the ground, at the bullring, which was the ground, saw the whites of their little brown eyes, gave a quick wave, and dumped it out. Rick opened to one side and just a bit lower.

The smoke was a dud, wouldn't you know it, but I could see Efren and Adan make it two more 'in' *perfectamente.* Rick and I weaved in for the target. Rick on a PC, me on my Piglet. Both of us looked like we were in a good position to make it. Rick hooked in beautifully. I started in—no brakes, no wind, no low turns.

I ended up just outside the ring. Oh well, five out of six of us got in ... but why me?

People were coming from everywhere, helping me back into the ring. Then the six of us joined up in the ring. The crowd went wild. After a few minutes of the limelight we exited to the stands for some liquid refreshment and were met by O'Leary, who had patiently acted as ground control and guardian of the moonshine.

I guess that sort of explains what and how and who had gotten into this thing, so my story continues…

I tensed for the first pass, dangling the cape off to my left. The cape is the key, I remembered. You move the cape, not yourself. "Aha, Toro, Aha!"

I moved in closer. The bull's head dropped; then suddenly he rushed me. I shook the cape and he headed right for it. At the last instant I pulled it aside and he brushed on by me to the next 'Para-Matador.'

The contest between men and beast continued and we all became bolder. Chepe was first to grab the bull's tail and soon Adan, Efren and Hinchman were astride El Toro. The fight was becoming a circus.

Then it happened. O'Leary was moving in on the bull when he suddenly charged, goring Dan with his horn in the chest and throwing him back out of the way. We all froze. Dan stood clutching himself. Slowly he pulled his hand away and for a moment seemed afraid to look. Then his eyes slowly dropped to his chest … Nothing; no hole anyway.

He stiffened, drew himself up and charged the bull, his own head lowered now. He caught the bull near the shoulder, simultaneously grabbing his forefeet. The bull was down, successfully gored by an Irishman—undoubtedly a first in bullfight history. We all jumped on the bull and held him down as the crowd yelled, "El Gordo, El Gordo, El Gordo … Ole, El Gordo!" Dan O'Leary had been renamed.

That night we were the honored guests of the town of Juchitlan. We wined, dined, danced and sang around the town square with the entire populace until the last reveler went home and the long purple creepers of dawn streaked across the sky. Then we fell into our pick-up and headed back to Guadalajara.

Pound, Pound, Pound, Pound. "Hey 'Dirty Billy,' are you awake?"

"No, I'm having a nightmare; I must be!"

"Dirty Billy, it's me, Joe."

"Well," I said, "I guess I'm awake, what day is it?"

"Tomorrow." said Joe.

"That's what I was afraid of," said I. "What time is it?"

"Almost noon," from Joe. "Oh yeah, well look, I know I said I'd teach you guys to jump at eight in the morning, so I guess it's too late to jump—so, Good night," I said.

"Too late to jump," said Joe, "but not too late to teach...right, Teach?"

"I was afraid you'd think of that. Why, just tell me, do you medical students have to be so smart? Why can't you be dumb? OK, let's go—is everyone here?" I asked, trying to hide a monster green hangover in the closet.

"Yeah, since eight. How'd the jump and bullfight go?" inquired Joe.

"I think we won, but I'm guessing. Some little rascal named Tequila has been putting funny notions in my head lately."

Our jump stories and rap sessions of the last three days had generated enough interest with Rick's classmates that five of them had decided to make their first jumps. So we began First Jump Course, Mexican-Style: five students, a T-10 with a Stevens Cutaway System, reserve, blackboard, tree limb for malfunction procedures, and a pickup truck for PLFs.

By five o'clock that afternoon I was amazed. After training hundreds of students, I found that this was the best group I had ever been associated with. Here they were doing their own critiques, pin checks, and packing. After an oral exam, we broke class for the day and prepared for the morning.

We got an early start for Magdalena Airport near the town of Tequila (God, that's a popular place) with hopes of renting an air taxi to put our students out of. We were in luck, and in a short time we had the door off a battered 206, marked a target in a nearby pasture with a cheapo canopy, and put O'Leary to work holding the windsock on the DZ.

Luckily we managed to borrow another canopy and reserve from the Mexican Army bunch, rig up another Stevens System, and *Voila!* we began jumping our students two at a time, Rick and I both jump-mastering. Each pass brought more and more spectators until the field was nearly full of kids, farmhands, and interested bystanders—whuffos, Latin-style.

The last Show of the Gringo Barnstormers drew to an end as late afternoon descended with the last student and a two-man over Tequila. We packed ourselves, our students, cerveza and tequila into the pickup and headed off into the sunset. Five new brothers had been initiated into the sky. "Adios until next year!"

Billy Bishop

<u>Note:</u> *Billy Bishop (Dirty Billy, as his friends knew him) was killed in an automobile accident near Guadalajara, Mexico, on September 15, 1976.*

Party In Paradise

I was at the 1977 Thanksgiving skydiving meet at Zephyrhills, near Tampa, Florida, when Jim "Whitey" Whiting told me he was planning a New Year's "Party In Paradise" skydiving adventure in Hawaii and asked if I'd like to attend and write an article about it for our *Star Crest Magazine.*

Free room and board for a week sounded good to me, plus I'd always wanted to go to Hawaii. Lots of my friends had already been several times, and at 36, time was ticking.

On the flight over I was reading Hal Lindsay's *"Satan Is Alive And Well On Planet Earth"* and was intrigued by the part that said that earthbound and demon spirits resided in the depths of the earth, and that the Mariana Trench, one of the deepest places in the ocean, had an abnormal amount of paranormal activity and mysterious disappearances on its surface.

The Party In Paradise was held on Oahu's North Shore. Dillingham Airfield was where the skydiving was taking place, and about a mile farther west, just before the paved road ended at Kaena Point, was Camp Erdman where we skydivers were housed.

Camp Erdman—the skydivers called it Camp Wierdman—was a YMCA camp with a huge recreation hall and swimming pool right on the beach. Directly across the road were the cabins and right behind the cabins, rugged green mountains rose steeply to a couple thousand feet. The scenery was fantastic.

The skydivers shared the recreation hall with middle school Japanese students during the day. I could sense the culture contrast, as did the Japanese instructors, but the skydivers seemed oblivious. As the Japanese kids were singing Disney type songs like *"It's A Small, Small World"* on the first floor, heavy metal music blared from the P.A. speakers in the chow hall on the second floor where the skydivers ate, drank, and partied. There were some concerned looks from the Japanese instructors, but they never said anything.

All of the cabins but one housed skydivers from various parts of the mainland. Most groups from a certain place were housed together. I missed my original flight and arrived a day late, so I got the empty cabin. That was a good thing in that I had privacy and wouldn't be kept awake by a bunch of rowdy skydivers wanting to party all night.

One cabin in particular housed a bunch from the New York and Chicago areas. I noticed at certain times all the lights would be off, it would be quiet, and no one would answer the door. I found my way in one afternoon and tried to socialize with them. But they soon became obnoxious, insulting and slightly hostile, so I left. I began to suspect that they were Satanists holding rituals and sex orgies.

About the third night we had a party on the beach with a bonfire under the palm trees. I had downed a few beers when someone passed me some Hawaiian weed. I took a hit and passed it on, knowing it was about ten times more potent than weed from the mainland.

After a while another late-comer showed up. He had just flown in from Washington State to meet his sister who was already there. This guy (I'll call him Don) was very loud and brassy. He had brought a stash of cocaine with him and was running around turning people on and exclaiming "Cocaine is God, cocaine is God."

I snorted a line and not too long afterward, fell off the log I was sitting on. This generated a lot of laughs because at the time, I was considered to be pretty hard core. I decided it was time to pack it in before I embarrassed myself any further, so I bid goodnight amid hoots and howls, and made it back to my cabin.

Here's where things got interesting. I was feeling truly euphoric being in Hawaii, and as I lay on my bunk next to the louvered glass windows, I could hear the surf as a continuous roar. Not like the California surf where it ebbs, crescendos, splashes and hisses, but a continuous roar. I lapsed into a semiconscious state as the roar of the surf transcended into the most beautiful and intricate drumming I'd ever heard. I've been a conga drummer since my teens, and I'd never heard anything that rhythmic. I was unfamiliar with those rhythms and couldn't play them at the time, so why was I hearing them in my head?

I snapped out of my trance, and back came the roar of the waves. I thought, *"Wow that was great. Let's see if I can do that again."* Sure enough, 1 was able to replace the roar of the breaking waves with the drums. After about the third time, I began to get a little flippant, thinking *"Hey, I can do this any time I want."*

Just then, right through the wall facing the mountains, marched five or six Hawaiian warriors from a time past. They were in full color, slightly transparent, carried spears and shields, and looked angry, although they didn't seem demonic. As they glided past my bunk their feet didn't appear to be touching the floor. They paused briefly, and one of them looked at me before they continued on out through the opposite wall.

I rose up in my bunk and said aloud, "This is bullshit!!"

As soon as I said that, a gust blew in from the louvered windows and kicked up a grayish whirlwind, blowing dust and debris at the foot of my bunk. Seeing this psychic phenomena, backed up by a physical manifestation, convinced me it was real and I cried "Jesus, help me" as I pulled the blanket over my head. As soon as I said "Jesus, help me," the whirlwind dissipated and blew out the window. I was scared and lay there wondering what the hell had just happened. I hadn't been to church in years and wasn't in the habit of calling on Jesus. But it worked!

Enter Don, who as a late-comer also got a bunk in the spare cabin. His bunk was on the other side of the room from mine and in between us was the bathroom and shower, so even though I couldn't see him, I could hear him. It was about 2:00 a.m. and Don, who had previously been running around crowing "Cocaine is God," was tossing and turning in his bunk, retching and moaning that something was after him and he wanted to go back home. He'd been in Hawaii for the first time for only a few hours.

By that time I knew what was going on: the spirits were harassing Don, but he couldn't see them as I had. So I went over to his bunk and said "Take it easy, partner. You'll be OK, you just have island fever."

But he insisted, "No, I've got to get out of here now! Get Whitey up and get me to the airport!"

So that's what I did—at 3:00 a.m. Whitey was in his private cabin with his girlfriend. He didn't like it. But Don was stressing so bad, Whitey decided it was better to drive him to the Honolulu airport than to have him running around freaking out at the Party In Paradise.

I cautiously told a couple of skydivers about my experience, and their reaction was that I had gotten too stoned. However, when I asked a few native Hawaiians, they told me that spirit sightings were not uncommon in the islands and that other people (mainly locals) had seen basically the same scenario as I had in the area. One local asked if the spirit had looked at me. When I answered "Yes, but briefly," he looked concerned and said, "If they look at you, the legend says that you will die."

Well, I didn't die, but I did have an extraordinary run of bad luck for the next 20 years.

Three years later, on December 6, 1981, Whitey and some of his local skydiving friends—most of whom had attended the Party In Paradise boogies in 1978, 1979 and 1980—were to make an exhibition jump into a football game at Aloha Stadium next to Pearl Harbor.

The 12-place Twin Beech stalled in a tight turn over the stadium at a low altitude, rolled, and crashed upside down next to the Arizona Memorial in Pearl Harbor. Only one guy bailed out in time to survive. The rest were all killed, including Whitey, sitting in the front seat with the pilot. I interviewed the sole survivor, a 19-year-old, by telephone from his hospital bed in Honolulu. His account of the crash and what he saw afterward was horrific.

This is what he told me:

"I was sitting in the door, with two others behind me. We got a call from the ground that half-time hadn't started yet and we needed to circle for awhile. The pilot was the drop zone operator's youngest son, who was just learning to fly the Twin Beech. He got too tight in a turn and the Beech stalled.

"We were at 3,500 feet when the left wing dropped and we rolled. I wanted to jump, but Byron Black (the drop zone owner sitting against the bulkhead up front) yelled to stay in the plane. His reasoning was that the aircraft would be harder to control if everyone started exiting.

"Everyone stayed put until we went into a spin and then I jumped, pulled my main, got line stretch and hit the water. The two guys behind me fired their reserves, but didn't open in time and bounced in the water. My leg was broken from hitting the Beech's tail, but I could wade in the chest-deep water.

"It was getting dark, but I tread water over to the two guys who had left behind me and they were both dead. The Beech was only about 100 yards away, crashed upside down with the open door and tail sticking up out of the water.

"I looked in to see if anyone was still alive. All I could see was just a jumbled bunch of helmets, boots, heads, arms and legs all melded together like a giant ball of flesh."

After the interview I told him that I had seen my share of grisly accidents and bounces, but if it were me, I'd probably have skipped looking in the plane, knowing they'd all have to be dead and mangled going in at 200 mph. I suggested that he was numbed by shock, and he agreed.

On my last visit there in 1984, I overheard some of the guys at a party talking about how ironic it was that a month or so before the crash Whitey had made a mock recording, with sound effects and screams, of the Beech crashing in the ocean off Kaena Point. They played it for me. It was chilling and prophetic.

My mind flashed back to the first Party In Paradise when I was walking along a road by the beach and Whitey picked me up in his car. When I got in, he said, "Hi Newell, how does it feel to be dead?"

I replied rather irritated, "What the hell are you talking about? I'm not dead!"

He said, "Oh yes you are, but you don't know it. Look around. You're in paradise!"

Bill Newell

He Was *Not* Grinning

Man, sometimes I used to fly so much at the parachute center that I would be desperate to find and check out a new pilot. It seemed like I would fly for six months straight before some new guy showed up, and then I got a six-month break from flying so I could jump on the weekends instead.

It was late September; I had been through one of the flying stages and I was really getting tired of hauling the Cessna 195 and Beech 18 up to altitude and racing the jumpers down so I could do it all over again. The busy season was just about to arrive for us at the Gulch and I knew I had to find a pilot soon.

Eloy, Arizona, was about 20 miles southeast of Casa Grande and I remembered that the guy who ran the crop-spraying operation there had a son who was just breaking in as a spray pilot. Their season was about to slow down. I figured that boy was going to be looking for some flying time during the winter. He had a multi-engine rating and a lot of tail dragger time so he would be perfect for the 195, and then we could check him out in the Beech.

I wandered over to Eloy during the week in the 195 to see if I could talk to him. But I knew that I would first have to convince the old man that his son would be safe. The 195 was as clean as I could get her, for a jump plane. I knew the old man was going to look her over carefully.

I gave him my best sales pitch about how safely we tried to operate and said I would keep the kid away from the skydivers when he wasn't flying so he wouldn't be tempted to start jumping and partying with our more rambunctious types on the drop zone.

He wasn't much impressed and especially didn't want the boy around our hell-raising crowd, but he knew the kid wanted to fly and could use a little experience before the cotton season started the following summer. Surprisingly, he agreed to come over the next weekend and take a look at our operation. That wasn't exactly what I wanted to hear, but I didn't have much choice. We had a group of jumpers coming from Southern California and some from Salt Lake City; it promised to be a busy weekend but if I could keep the old crop duster and his son occupied, they might not get too cozy with the jumpers and maybe I would still get my pilot for the winter.

The weather on Saturday turned out to be nasty for the Sonora Desert. The wind was blowing and the overcast was down to about a thousand feet. The forecast was for improving ceilings in the afternoon so everyone was sitting around waiting for a break in the weather. Everyone except: dEd Dugan.

dEd was an F-100 instructor pilot out of Tucson; he commuted up to Casa Grande every Friday or Saturday in his trusty old Cessna 170 to jump with us. dEd, like most fighter pilots, was easily bored so instead of sitting around, he proceeded to treat everyone to a low-level aerobatic performance in his commuter plane. It was a masterful performance. I stood outside the hangar and watched him roll and loop and hammerhead up into and back out of the clouds.

dEd was doing things in the 170 that you wouldn't think possible. He had the right door off in case we needed the extra lift that weekend, but he was the only one in the plane. Just as dEd disappeared into the overcast in a vertical climb during a loop, I felt—more than saw—two people walk up and stand beside me, watching the demonstration.

The 170 reappeared out of the overcast, still vertical, but this time in the opposite direction. IT WAS AWESOME! I looked down for a moment to see who might be standing beside me and there he was—my new pilot, grinning from ear to ear, enjoying the heck out of the show. Problem was sonny's Dad was also standing there, and he was *not* grinning.

I wasn't too worried; as soon as I explained that dEd was an experienced combat fighter pilot just back from the 'Nam, and a man with that kind of experience knew exactly what he was doing, he would have to agree it was perfectly safe.

For a nanosecond, the old man's frown moderated somewhat but then he looked me in the eye and told me in no uncertain terms that he had to follow the rules in his business and, "That there fighter pilot should damn well know better than anyone that he shouldn't be doing that in a Cessna 170 and at that altitude."

I was thinking that some people just don't get it and that this might be a little harder sale than I had first thought. I saw that Ed was leveling out from the loop; he throttled back like he was finished and would land. I was hoping that the last loop was the only part of the show the old crop duster and his boy had seen.

I decided to change tack a little, and I told the old man he was right. I would have to talk to dEd about what he had done and ask him not to do it again. In the meantime, dEd was circling around to the south, obviously lining up for a buzz job through the drop zone full of cheering skydivers. dEd leveled off at about 25 feet and I was relieved that this would be a conservative buzz job, not the usual "two feet off the sage brush" with skydivers diving for the sand to save their butts from getting ground up in the prop.

Just as I was about to begin my final sales pitch to my new pilot's father, a loud roar of applause and approval rose from the delighted crowd of observers.

I looked up at dEd, but no one was in the pilot's seat! I couldn't help but double over laughing and guffawing loudly as I saw the 170 go by. dEd was standing sideways where the right seat would have been. His left hand was wrapped around the seatbelt, flying with his right hand, and his head turned to the right so he could watch where he was going. It was quite a feat of airmanship, especially when as he flew past us I could see his pants peeled down to his ankles and his bare ass hanging out the open door. It's a moon I'll never forget or probably ever see again. I couldn't stop laughing and had to hold onto the hangar to keep from falling on the ramp and rolling over and over. The things you get to see in this crowd just CRACK ME UP!

Oh dear!! I remembered all of a sudden that my new pilot and his old man saw the same thing. I wondered if the old fart would crack a smile after seeing that! Unfortunately I'll never know the answer, but I can guess. When I looked around to check on them they were nowhere to be found. I saw a large dust cloud rising from an old pickup truck exiting the airport as fast as it would go—heading, I assumed, back to Eloy and the safety of home.

As the overcast began to break up I headed over to the old Beech and began pulling the props through and checking her out, all the time cursing that damn Dugan. I ought to make him fly jumpers all damn weekend, but there he is, his usual handsome smile and his parachute strapped on, waiting for me to crawl into the left seat. I was going to have to look elsewhere for my new pilot.

Michael D. Larson

Clueless

In 1966 at the Houston Skydivers, only a water jump stood between us and completing the requirements for a 'D' license. Gary Lewis held FAI 'B' license #5561and I held 'C' #1798. We wanted the 'D' or "Expert Parachutist" rating for competition and unrestricted parachuting activities. To become 'D' qualified, the U.S. Parachute Association mandated a parachute water landing. Therein lies a NSTIWTIWGD tale.

Yes, we knew water jumps were fundamentally dangerous. In the '60s, water jumps were a popular way to die. For several many jumpers (say 5-15 per year) it was their last jump. But we *knew* that risks wouldn't pertain to *us*. It was male logic: clear and simple. Clueless and bullet-proof.

Such "hazardous landing" skydives are not simple to set up. So when friends helped us round up a jump plane and pilot, we jumped at the opportunity to make our required water jump into nearby Lake Houston. Unavoidably, water jumps involve bizarre sites using unfamiliar gear. Plus you land in deep wet water. Your parachutes get soaked, you gotta hassle with air-drying, and the reserve repack in those days cost $15.00. That was big money—equal to four skydives, food for five days, or beer for two. Big money. Grumble.

From 7,200 feet AGL, Lake Houston is too big to miss and plenty wet. Dammed up, the West Fork of the San Jacinto River spreads over 11,854 acres. That is one big-ass lake. Pre-jump, we had a serious safety briefing wherein jump pilot Carlos (C.G.) Wallace (D-152) declared, "OK, I'm only doing this as a favor…I want you guys to NOT fuck up! OK?"

Cool. We were Spartan cowboys, wearing B4 backpack rigs, bathing suits and T-shirts, but neither shoes nor helmets. For main parachutes we borrowed 28-foot, 'flat' round 1.1 C9 student canopies. Like everyone, we carried chest-mounted 24-foot round reserve parachutes.

A goal of water jumps is to not get snared by shroud lines or canopy whilst they submerge to the lake's bottom. Triumph here means shedding your sinking parachute's harness in advance of drowning. To mitigate that risk, I would jump with my leg-straps fully extended. Niceties such as flotation gear or a pick-up boat seemed superfluous. I'm a good swimmer; plus there were plenty of boats on the lake. We'd hitchhike a ride back to land. No big deal. Our jumpmates Hop, Hawk-eye, and Nasty agreed to meet up with us onshore for the car ride back to the Crosby DZ.

On a Houston day with 98-degree (F) on the thermostat and humidity at 98 percent, Carlos dumped Gary and me over the lake. A thoughtful lad, I had reckoned that wearing a reserve parachute was expensive and uncalled-for, because a 1.1 canopy hardly ever malfunctioned. Plus, you have to be going over 70 MPH before water-impact is permanently fatal. I thought it was worth the risk.

Our reserve parachutes abandoned in the airplane, we exited over Lake Houston for a 30-second delayed fall. With no altimeter and no stopwatch, I eyeballed the big-ass lake. In freefall my too-loose rig flapped around on my skinny frame like a sheet in the wind. A novel experience, that …

Meanwhile, there was a *huge* body of water clearly headed my way. Durn … too vast, it conveyed zippo altitude clues. So I counted the time elapsed: "Er … X-thousand, another thousand, Y-thousand … Something thousand…Umm…"

I got to the count of "Plenty Something!" when the tree line-lake horizon rocketed up. This was my indication that an open canopy would be indispensable for operational success. I promptly deployed my parachute. Opening shock smacked my gonads, "Whomp!" *(Moan…)* With leg straps loose, the control lines were WAY up the risers, requiring monkey-like climbing to reach them.

I undid my chest strap, per plan, pre-landing. I hit the water, went under, and raised my arms like "I surrender" to shuck the parachute. I paddled away unentrapped, then circled back and snuck up on the sinking canopy, found the apex bridle cord, and swam away with it on a leash that wasn't attached to me. Just like I planned.

Then I took a look around … *Hmmn … no boats thereabout!* This was *not* per plan. Yelling and arm-waves suckered in a skiff with two fishermen. "Howdy!"

After a nice conversation about the fishing and their day so far, they proceeded to motor-away. "WAIT!" More conversation ensued. "You don't have friends on the lake to pick you up???!"

We discussed that; it was a short conversation. "Please …"

"So … OK, we give you a ride?" My answer: "Yes, Sir, Please! I'd appreciate that!"

I clambered aboard and we hauled in my rig. Parachutes are giant sea anchors; this one must have weighed a ton. It took all three of us to get the water-logged gear into the boat. We trundled to shore where I disembarked to discover that bare feet, shoreline, mud, and heavy rig impeded my progress to Zero MPH.

My pals yawned and waved from the beach. Gary had somehow hijacked a ride, too, and came ashore. Laid back on the lakeshore was our stalwart ground crew. They thoughtfully said, "Well, OK … Crazy Pat, what say we grab a beer or two on the way back to the DZ?"

Pat Works

The World's First Skydiving Chicken

Here is the story of the "World's First Skydiving Chicken" and how I and the Jump Maine Skydivers almost got lynched for that little stunt which took place in Maine over 25 years ago. I have been referred to as "Chicken Bob" for my delinquent participation in the event.

Pittsfield, Maine, is a small community with a population of approximately 4,500. It was once the Poultry Capital of the region, and every July there is an event called the Pittsfield Egg Festival. The Egg Festival is a homecoming of sorts for former residents. In those days it was a three-day event that featured a huge chicken barbecue, crafts, carnival rides, and the world's largest omelet. The size of that frying pan still amazes me.

There was live music and dancing on Saturday night, and an airshow complete with flour bombing contests, vintage aircraft, stunt pilots and yes, the Jump Maine Skydivers, a hearty group of characters bent on chasing women, drinking and, of course, jumping out of airplanes, especially in front of crowds—even more so enthusiastically when there might be the possibility of getting in the newspapers and on TV.

Our role was to jump once on Friday evening and five times on Saturday. For this we were furnished with money to pay for the aircraft, copious amounts of beer, all the food we wanted, and lots of publicity. Naturally we got lots of attention from the women, especially on Saturday night when we showed up at the dance in our tan chinos and shirts smartly emblazoned with the "Jump Maine Skydivers" logo.

One year we added a little attraction to our show by taking the mascot of the festival—you guessed it, a live chicken named Amanda—up in a gym bag and bailing out with the bag, chicken and all, from 5,000 feet. The jumper who got to do the honors was chosen by drawing the short straw the previous Saturday at the end of the day's jumping, which was essentially the transition from skydiving to drinking beer around the fire where we camped at the Drop Zone.

The ill-fated stunt was announced over the local radio station and on the P.A. system at the start of the festival. Amanda's annual jump was always a big hit with the crowds, especially the kids. On landing, the lucky skydiver opened the gym bag and out popped Amanda, none the less for wear after her 3,000-foot freefall. The press would be there snapping photos of the jumper and the hapless chicken which was then sent back to her cage where she had to endure another day of rubber-necked geeks staring and poking at her through the wire.

A nerve-wracking jump must have been a welcome relief to the duties she had to put up with during the entire festival.

In 1980, after a hard day of skydiving, I was relaxing around the fire with the rest of this group of yahoos when I came up with the idea of cutting approximately six feet from the top of an old T-10 and leaving about eight feet of suspension line which was to be tied to a large, mesh onion bag in which the chicken would be placed and dropped from an altitude of 500 to 600 feet. Then Amanda would truly be the "World's First Skydiving Chicken."

A few more beers by everyone, and her fate was sealed. I went to work the next morning and cut her parachute from an old T-10 that we had used for first-jump students. During the week I attached the onion bag to it and put in a piece of wood that we figured to weigh as much as the average chicken. I didn't bother too much with fine rigging or any other technical stuff.

After enough beer to give me the courage to climb the 250-foot-high local water tower, I test-dropped the rig from the top rung of the ladder. It worked like a charm. This was gonna be one famous chicken and we were gonna be the famous skydivers who dropped her.

I was the self-appointed PR man for our little stunt. For the next two weeks I contacted newspapers and radio stations to tell them about the Jump Maine Skydivers and how we were going to introduce Amanda to the world of freefall parachuting at 2:00 p.m. on the Saturday of the Pittsfield Egg Festival. It was gonna be BIG!

We arrived at the festival on Friday night and jumped before a huge crowd. The radio station was there, announcing our presence over the air. It had a powerful P.A. system at the fairgrounds that broadcast the station's music and announcements to festival-goers as well listeners elsewhere, and was scheduled to be there for the entire festival. I got in a little airtime and explained the mission that Amanda was going to undertake the next day, describing it as a perilous, heroic deed to be done for the entertainment of the people at the Pittsfield Egg Festival.

On Saturday we made three jumps into the fairgrounds, which were right across the road from the Pittsfield Airport from which we flew. The night before the event we had drawn straws for the ground crew/announcer slot; I lost out but Hell, I was having fun.

Around 1:30 p.m. I went on the air and over the P.A. system to proudly announce how Amanda would boldly go where no other chicken had gone before. I told the crowd and the listeners at home that the plane with the world's first skydiving chicken was just lifting off at the Pittsfield Airport and would soon be overhead.

This gave new meaning to the term "Whuffo."

Soon the black and white Cessna 172 with the door removed for skydiving was over the crowd at about 500 feet. The plan was to make a pass over the fairgrounds at this altitude, head back into the wind, and unload the chicken into the prop blast. I explained every detail—how we conducted serious research and made numerous, highly technical drop tests to ensure the success of Amanda's first jump.

The plane turned into the wind at the far end of the fairgrounds. I could see the jumper (who shall remain nameless for fear of reprisal from animal rights groups) in the door spotting the jump. The crowd was silent as I explained the fine art of jump mastering. All eyes strained skyward as the parachute carrying not just the world's first parachuting fowl but the one and only Amanda, reigning mascot of the widely acclaimed Pittsfield, Maine Egg Festival, exited the aircraft into the blue void.

The radio announcer excitedly cried out: "There she is, folks! Amanda, the skydiving chicken!"

I watched the canopy twist and knot into a flapping streamer, the helpless chicken descending at a rate of speed that insured high impact with the ground. I switched off the microphone, told the radio guy that all was not good at that moment up in the Wild Blue, and suggested that he go to a commercial or play some music. *"Blood on The Risers"* would have been fitting at that moment.

That bird was burning a hole in the atmosphere. She barreled toward the grassy landing area where we had, in our beer-induced calculations, figured she would softly settle in front of a cheering crowd beneath a fully inflated parachute.

Poor ol' Amanda smacked the tar walkway in front of the dismal crowd, bounced about five feet, and came to rest, still flapping in the onion bag. People screamed, children cried, some laughed, and many were shocked. I decided it was time to bail out of there. My exit through the angry crowd was not made any easier by my nice maroon t-shirt with the jump club logo on it. What I would have given for a burlap sack to hide in at that moment.

I hustled to my car with the skydiving bumper stickers, one of which stated *"Skydivers Go Down Faster"* and included a United States Parachute Association decal, in the rear window. As far I was concerned, my jump buddies were on their own. If they were smart, they would get out of there quickly. I felt no guilt about abandoning them under fire. After all, I was the one whose name would be all over the newspapers for cruelty to chickens. There was no honor among us juvenile delinquent reprobates on that fateful day!

As I inserted the key into the door lock, figuring I just might escape a lynching, a farmer came up to me asking if I was "one o' them there sky-jumpin' fools who dropped that poor chicken out of that airy-plane."

I said, "Yes sir, but I can explain."

He cut me off abruptly, stating: "Sonny, there ain't no explanation fer wantin' to jump outta good airy-plane, an' even less for droppin' a chicken outta one. You best git outta here before the same thing happens to you!"

Point taken! I bailed out of there and decided to affiliate myself with another jump club downstate for the next few weekends while things calmed down.

I later learned that Amanda was taken out behind one of the fairground buildings, put out of her misery, then placed on the grill over the barbecue pit and sold as freshly grilled chicken.

One of the club members who lived in Pittsfield just happened to be running for election to the Maine State Legislature that coming November. Immediately after our debacle, much of his time was spent writing letters of apology to the festival organizers, the local Chamber of Commerce, and the public at large. He still got elected. Unlike me, his association with the death-defying chicken (who failed miserably at her task) was soon forgotten.

For years afterward, every time I showed up at another drop zone, I was greeted with "Hey, Lane, bounced any chickens lately?"

Bob Lane

No Shit, I Remember When You Nearly Died

A dreadful time and place for a high-visibility fuck-up is your own RW Camp.

My second book, *"United We Fall,"* had just been published in 1978. I had a knack for training others by sharing discoveries: no-contact, Skydance, relaxation and attitude are sure paths to flight for the joy of flying. With my wife, Jan, we initiated a paradigm shift in the skydive experience.

I tagged along on one jump at Perris with Jan as training-reviewer and coach-coach. After her stick had a good class skydive, I saw that Jan and I were in the same quadrant tracking off. She could not pull out the pilot chute. It was jammed, caught, stuck under the flap. Her mindset and focus were on pulling more vigorously. Meanwhile, we sailed through 2,500 feet. Time seemed to slow down as we sailed through 2,000 ... 1,800 ... then 1,700 feet.

She was still working to yank it out. Altitude was unwinding inexorably ... tick-tock, like a clock. Now, Jan's green gear was painted onto the ground and burned into my mind. *Please pull!*

Not wanting to see her bounce, I blinked my eyes. At 1,200 feet, I had to go. I pulled and as my canopy was opening, to my wonderment she was still in sight. She plummeted to 700 feet. This was grim business; I did not want to watch my wife die. I'd blink my eyes, recheck, and blink... check.... Surely she was way below 500 feet by now. Soon she would hit, and instantly ... I blinked and checked ... it was a bad scene.

Finally, there was Jan on the ground, her reserve lying around her. As I set up to land I could see her hop up to stomp around in circles howling, "Oh Bugger!! Damn! Damn!"

I landed close by and asked, "Hey Kiddo, so, what's going on?"

She was angry that she'd dropped her reserve ripcord and would never find it. This was a case-of-beer infraction, of course. I said, "Jan, Baby, ah, you opened really low; your reserve handle must be nearby."

She said, "No way!"

I said, "We'll find it."

We looked around and both of us spotted it at the same time. Fifteen feet away, her ripcord was decorating a bush.

Not having anything clever to say, I kept silent for once. She arm-wrapped the reserve as the DZ truck zoomed up. I don't recollect our actually talking to each other.

But on the ride back, Jan remarked, "Shit! Oh shit, that was low! Wow! Ground rush big time! Dumb! Damn! I hope nobody saw the stupid stunt I just pulled."

Back at the packing area, skydivers surrounded her, reacting to the adrenalin rush of seeing a fleeting canopy, excited, delighted, happy and pumped up that Jan was not dead. She did look rather green and awful. On the other hand, another 30 to 40 percent imagined Jan's body behind the parked DC-3 where she had landed.

Years later, Jan's stunt continued to elicit remarks like "Howdy! Whoo! Boy! I recall when you nearly bounced ... No Shit! ... Thought you were dead!"

Pat Works

RW Underground Publishing Company
1656 Beechwood Ave.
Fullerton, CA USA 92835

Made in the USA
Middletown, DE
21 December 2019